Amateurs, Professionals, and Serious Leisure

Amateurs, Professionals, and Serious Leisure

ROBERT A. STEBBINS

McGill-Queen's University Press
Montreal & Kingston • London • Buffalo

© McGill-Queen's University Press 1992
ISBN 0–7735–0901–1

306.48
S81a

Legal deposit second quarter 1992
Bibliothèque nationale du Québec

Printed in Canada on acid-free paper

This book has been published with the help of a grant
from the Social Science Federation of Canada, using
funds provided by the Social Sciences and Humanities
Research Council of Canada. Publication has also been
supported by the University Endowment Fund,
University of Calgary.

Canadian Cataloguing in Publication Data

Stebbins, Robert A., 1938–
    Amateurs, professionals and serious leisure
    Includes bibliographical references and index.
    ISBN 0-7735-0901-1
    1. Leisure – Social aspects. 2. Professional employees.
    3. Amateurism.   4. Work – Social aspects.
    I. Title.
    GV14.45.S83 1992   306.4'812   C92-090091-7

Typeset in 10/12 Palatino by Nancy Poirier Typesetting,
Ottawa.

To Max Kaplan

Contents

Acknowledgments

I wish to thank both the University of Calgary and the Killam Trusts for the Killam Residential Fellowship granted to me in the fall of 1990 for the purpose of completing this book. Without the reduction in teaching and administrative responsibilities made possible by this award, the manuscript would have languished indefinitely in its gestation. As important to the process of scholarly communication was the publication grant received from the Social Science Federation of Canada, using funds provided by the Social Science and Humanities Research Council of Canada. That subvention is gratefully acknowledged.

Because this book is a synthesis of fifteen years of research, portions of some of my initial publications have been incorporated here, albeit with considerable change and elaboration to the original texts. The most extensive passages come from the following sole-authored publications: "Amateurism and Postretirement Years." *Journal of Physical Education and Recreation* (*Leisure Today* supplement) 49 (October 1978): 40–1; *Amateurs: On the Margin Between Work and Leisure*, Beverly Hills, California: Sage, 1979; "'Amateur' and 'Hobbyist' as Concepts for the Study of Leisure Problems," *Social Problems* 27 (1980): 413–17; and "Serious Leisure: A Conceptual Statement." *Pacific Sociological Review* 25 (1982): 251–72.

Mention should be made of William Reeves and Mary Thompson, who read parts of the manuscript; our subsequent discussions resulted in several important changes. Also, I wish most sincerely to thank Carolyn Andres, who persisted with utmost effectiveness in typing a clean manuscript from what was, at times, a nearly impenetrable copy, and Wendy Dayton, whose careful editorial work is evident throughout.

Introduction

If I had to identify one day on which the fifteen-year project reported on in this book commenced, I would have to select a day in early January of 1974. For it was during that month that I began the library research that eventually led to a paper on amateur musicians for presentation at a conference the following spring. Having been involved in amateur music for most of my life (except for a two-year interlude as a professional), I was well aware that participants in that field considered amateurism to be something special. That January day marked my first academic opportunity to study amateur music systematically and to record some of my thoughts that had been collecting on the subject over the years.

My plan was to write an ethnographic paper on amateur classical musicians, based on my own experience as well as the biographic, autobiographic, and philosophic literature that touches on musicians' social lives. That I did. In fact, I wrote and subsequently published three papers. Yet, as far as this book is concerned, these were the least significant events in those early months of 1974.

What was most significant was my realization that neither sociology nor any other discipline had developed a substantial definition of amateur.[1] I discovered this lack during my search for a definition with which to organize my ideas and observations on music amateurs. The search was in vain. Nevertheless, it compelled me to meet the problem head-on; to develop my own definitions of amateur – the results of which comprise much of chapter 3 of the present book. But there were other consequences as well.

The lack of a social science definition of amateurs meant that no one had actually conceived of them in the light in which they are examined here: as adults in a unique, marginal position within contemporary North American society. To be sure, amateur groups have been studied, but their status as amateurs in the community has never been the object of these investigations. Moreover, the groups have nearly always consisted of adolescents or children, for whom the consequences of pursuing a form of serious leisure differ greatly from those for adults.

It became clear, too, that amateurs are found throughout science, art, sport, and entertainment; that they can be distinguished, by a variety of criteria, from professionals who work in the same field and from dabblers who merely play at it; and that we need to know much more about seemingly one of the most complicated and neglected facets of modern leisure. So I set to work to design a major research project, one that would help answer many of the questions raised by my theoretical efforts.

By the spring of 1975, I had obtained the necessary funding to conduct an exploratory study of amateurism in the Dallas-Fort Worth area. It was a one-year project centring on amateurs in theatre, archaeology, and baseball. From it I learned that it was a mistake to study amateurs to the exclusion of their professional counterparts. I also learned that, if my exploration were to have true scientific value, I would have to study at least two examples in each of the aforementioned areas in which amateurs and professionals exist and are linked to one another. By the end of 1976, then, I had completed the first four of this octet of studies. This included my own participant-observation examination of the world of amateur classical music and a review of over 200 biographic, autobiographic, and philosophic accounts for a field in which, unlike the other seven studies, I was a "complete-member-researcher" (Adler and Adler 1987).

After my move to the University of Calgary, I launched into a similar exploration of Canadian astronomers, but this time at both levels. That study was conducted from late 1977 through early 1978. Then came my first contact with amateurs and professionals in the entertainment field. That was in the first half of 1979, when I undertook the study of magicians. Later, in 1983 and 1984, I returned to the field to examine a second sport: Canadian football. Later still came the study of stand-up comics, my second and final entertainment field. These later studies, unlike the first four, were based exclusively on Canadian samples.

All these studies, along with two theoretical statements, form the basis for the generalizations contained in this book – the final phase of this fifteen-year project. Rather than clutter each chapter with citations to specific printed reports, I have listed them below, by group, and then referenced them fully in the Bibliography. From here on, I shall discuss the groups themselves as well as combinations of these groups, more generally, under the heading of "the Project."

THEORETICAL STATEMENTS
"The Amateur: Two Sociological Definitions," *Pacific Sociological Review*
"Serious Leisure: A Conceptual Statement," *Pacific Sociological Review*

CLASSICAL MUSICIANS
"Music Among Friends: The Social Network of Amateur Classical Musicians," *International Review of Sociology* (Series II)
"Classical Music Amateurs: A Definitional Study," *Humboldt Journal of Social Relations*
"Creating High Culture: The American Amateur Classical Musician," *Journal of American Culture*

ACTORS AND ACTRESSES
Amateurs: On the Margin Between Work and Leisure
"Family, Work, and Amateur Acting," In *Social Research and Cultural Policy*

ARCHAEOLOGISTS
Amateurs: On the Margin Between Work and Leisure
"Avocational Science: The Avocational Routine in Archaeology and Astronomy," *International Journal of Comparative Sociology*
"Science *Amators*? Rewards and Costs in Amateur Astronomy and Archaeology," *Journal of Leisure Research*

BASEBALL PLAYERS
Amateurs: On the Margin Between Work and Leisure

ASTRONOMERS
"Avocational Science: The Avocational Routine in Archaeology and Astronomy," *International Journal of Comparative Sociology*
"Science *Amators*? Rewards and Costs in Amateur Astronomy and Archaeology," *Journal of Leisure Research*
"Amateur and Professional Astronomers: A Study of Their Inter-relationships," *Urban Life*

ENTERTAINMENT MAGICIANS
The Magician: Career, Culture, and Social Psychology in a Variety Art

FOOTBALL PLAYERS
Canadian Football: The View from the Helmet

STAND-UP COMICS
The Laugh Makers: Stand-Up Comedy as Art, Business, and Life-Style

A number of people have asked why I chose this particular mix of fields. My justification is partly practical. For various reasons, both financial and academic, the studies had to be carried out close to home. I thus had to draw on fields that were sufficiently represented locally. But I also wanted to look at established amateur groups, so that initially, at least, the difficulties of becoming established could be avoided. They could always be scrutinized later. I further decided that, where possible, my focus would be on collective amateurism, as opposed to individual amateurism (for example, painting, writing, playing golf or tennis), so that I could examine the extensive effects of social interaction. Again, the individual forms could always be dealt with at some other time. Also, because I prefer to collect my own data, I could only study the groups in tandem. Finally, I decided I had to get away from music, with which I have an insider's familiarity, and study other fields that I knew initially only as an outsider. The amateur groups mentioned earlier met these diverse considerations.

The methodology throughout the project has been qualitative, the exploratory research approach initially set out by Glaser and Strauss (1967) and more recently elaborated by Glaser (1978) and Strauss (1987). In general, I first observed the routine activities of each amateur-professional combination extensively. As I became acquainted with their lifestyles, I embarked on lengthy, unstructured, face-to-face interviews, in most cases with samples of thirty amateur or professional respondents. To the extent their lives warranted, I asked similar questions of the respondents in all fields; I felt I would then be in a better position to generalize across them. Each field was unique, however, demanding some special observing, analyzing, interviewing, probing, and reporting of its distinctive aspects. The result was a "substantive grounded theory" (Glaser and Strauss 1967:33–35) of each field studied.

In this book I develop, in somewhat more abstract terms, a "formal grounded theory" (as Glaser and Strauss put it) of amateurs and professionals, based on the eight substantive fields. Since the study of serious leisure has only begun to take off in other parts of the world, this development is done predominantly, although not exclusively, with reference to North America.

Furthermore, because the history, observations, interview data, and research methods of the specific fields – say, entertainment magic or archaeology – are presented in the publications just mentioned, I have not reviewed them further here. Indeed, what concerns me now are the commonalities across and within each of the four areas (art, sport, science, and entertainment). One last point: I have used the heading of serious leisure, a theoretical framework that emerged out of my explorations of amateurs vis-à-vis hobbyists and career volunteers.

Amateurs, Professionals, and Serious Leisure

CHAPTER ONE

Serious Leisure

In an age in which the quest for spectator and sensual diversions dominates the world of leisure, the phrase "serious leisure" has a rather curious ring. Historically, at least, such wording is oddly contradictory, for seriousness has commonly been associated only with work, whereas leisure has been seen as the happy, carefree refuge from our earnest pursuit of money and the social standing supposedly provided by a paying job. But this view now appears to be losing ground. Current values and behaviour patterns in work and leisure hint at the presence of a serious orientation toward leisure among a significant proportion (albeit still a minority) of the population in today's postindustrial society. The likelihood is that this proportion will continue to grow, and for some time. Evidence for this trend comes from various sources.

A number of writers, among them Jenkins and Sherman (1979), Sherman (1986), and Veal (1987), envisage a major reduction in the amount of time the typical worker will devote to a job in the future. This reduction is partly accounted for by a projected decline in the number of jobs available at all levels of skill and training, a projection based on the assumption of a declining economy.[1] Jenkins and Sherman (1979, 123), for instance, forecast a 23.2 percent decline in jobs in Britain by the year 2003. As significant, however, is their (1979, 163–4) observation that tomorrow's workweek will decrease, leaving us not only with more leisure time on our hands than before, but with the problem of how to use it effectively:

We only get a significant block of leisure on retirement, and then are too old to enjoy many of the facilities that are available for the younger elements of society. This is surely absurd. What it means is that we are working to continue working, not to enjoy the fruits of the work-economy and what it can buy. Not all leisure activities have a price, however, and we deprive ourselves even of these by our insistence on working from 16 or 18 or 21, up to 60 or 65, in one continuous, hard stretch ... Leisure is not only rest or hedonistic enjoyment. Leisure activities can be constructive and rewarding for both the person and society in general, and whether this is in the nature of gardening or undertaking voluntary work amongst the old or handicapped young, or even making one's expertise available to another set of people, the principle remains the same.

Jenkins and Sherman go on to recommend four-day workweeks, three-week work months, extra vacation periods, sabbatical leaves, and job sharing as possible ways of optimizing our work and leisure in our own interest. Lefkowitz's (1979) interviews with a sample of Americans indicate that some of them are already expanding their leisure involvements by voluntarily accepting early retirement or unemployment.

Lefkowitz's (1979) findings, like those of many of his confrères, signal a change in attitude toward gainful employment, still another factor in the predicted reduction of time spent at work. His interviewees want to do things that fulfil their human potential, that develop them as persons. Increasingly, they are searching for this opportunity in their leisure time. Yankelovich (1981, 231) notes that the overwhelming majority of Americans are no longer prepared to restrict their personal self-fulfilment, while advancing the power and well-being of government and business as employees. Black (1991) provides a journalistic account of Canadians with similar orientations, whereas Jenkins (1986, 199) notes the loss of the appeal of work in Europe. Bosserman and Gagan (1972, 113–14) and Best (1973) are among the writers who note that leisure in postindustrial society is no longer seen as chiefly a means of recuperating from the travail of the job. Like Lefkowitz's and Yankelovich's respondents, they now see leisure as offering a prime opportunity for personal expression, enhancement of self-identity, and self-fulfilment. Seltzer and Wilson (1980) found that both men and women with incomes above the median, and men with incomes below the median, use more of their non-work time for self-development than do those outside these categories.

The proposition to emerge from these impressionistic and descriptive studies is that, increasingly, people are working primarily because they need the money to sustain their leisure interests, interests that consume a growing proportion of their waking hours. As Aristotle put it, "The end of labour is to gain leisure." Consider the three men in another study who chose careers in secretarial work. They argue that, with their subsequent clear-cut hours of employment, they are freed to write poetry or to take university courses (Brewer 1979).

But if leisure is to supersede work as a way of finding personal fulfilment, identity enhancement, self-expression, and the like, people must be careful to adopt those forms with the greatest payoff. The theme of this book is that we reach this goal by engaging in serious, rather than casual or unserious, leisure. Briefly, serious leisure can be defined as the systematic pursuit of an amateur, hobbyist, or volunteer activity that is sufficiently substantial and interesting for the participant to find a career there in the acquisition and expression of its special skills and knowledge. My aim in this chapter is to define, describe, and interrelate the three types of this leisure: amateurism, hobbyist pursuits, and career volunteering. They contrast with a bewildering array of casual forms, such as sitting at a football game, riding a roller coaster, taking an afternoon nap, watching television, observing a fireworks display, going on a picnic, and so on.

The theme just mentioned is in no way a denial of the fact that a small segment of the population will always find that their work and leisure have merged. For them, their work is as fulfilling and exciting as any leisure activity can ever be (Dunnette et al. 1973). Nevertheless, most people in the future will likely shift their "central life interest" (Dubin 1979) to some sort of leisure involvement.

Lest my emphasis on work versus non-work circumscribe attention, the reader should note that this treatment of serious leisure will also be applied from time to time to those who have no job and perhaps even no intention of seeking one (i.e., the retired, the occupationally disabled, even the wilfully and unwillfully unemployed). It depends on how leisure is defined. Some may view amateur or volunteer pursuits as something other than leisure – perhaps work or some other special category. For instance, Roadburg (1985, 107) found that whereas nearly nine percent of his retired subjects mentioned that volunteering was work; less than one percent defined it as leisure. Significantly, it was usually those who held paying jobs (part-time or temporary work taken on after they had retired from their lifework) who viewed volunteering as leisure.

THE NATURE OF SERIOUS LEISURE

Serious leisure is one form of general leisure, the definition of which has proved to be inordinately difficult. In this book, the activity treated as leisure follows the classification developed by Stanley Parker (1983, 8–9). All five of his categories are presented here so the reader will clearly understand what is included in, and excluded from, the subsequent discussion:

1 *Work, working time, sold time, subsistence time.* Although, as we have already seen, "work" has a wider meaning than employment, for the purpose of analyzing life space it is usually identified with earning a living. If an employee is on piece rates then it is "work," or more precisely the product of work, that he sells; if he is on time rates then he sells so much working time. However, these are both ways of measuring work and working time, and differ only in the way the remuneration is calculated. "Subsistence time" lays emphasis on the purpose of work to the employee, that is, enabling him and his dependents to subsist.

2 *Work-related time, work obligations.* Apart from actual working time, most people have to spend a certain amount of time travelling to and from the place of work, and in preparing or "grooming" themselves for work. In some cases, however, at least part of the travelling time may be regarded more as a form of leisure than as work-related; for example, time spent reading newspapers or books, chatting to fellow-travellers, or playing cards with them. Voluntary overtime and having a second job may also be regarded as related to the main working time rather than as part of it, as may activities in the no-man's land between work and leisure, such as reading on the subject of one's work when at home, attending conferences or trade union meetings which have a social as well as a work side, and so on.

3 *Existence time, meeting physiological needs.* This is the first of three non-work groups. We all have to spend a certain minimum of time on sleep and on the mechanics of living – eating, washing, eliminating, and so on. Beyond the minimum necessary for reasonably healthy living, extra time spent on these things may be more like a leisure activity. Eating for pleasure, taking extra care with one's appearance for a party or social occasion, sexual activity beyond the call of purely physiological need, are some examples which show that the line between the satisfaction of "existence" needs and leisure activities is not always easy to draw.

4 *Non-work obligations, semi-leisure.* Joffre Dumazedier (1967) has coined the term *semi-leisure* to describe "activities which, from the point of view of the individual, arise in the first place from leisure, but which represent in differing degrees the character of obligations." The obligations are usually to other people, but may be to non-human objects, such as pets or homes or gardens. Again, the line between obligation and leisure is not always clear and depends to a large extent on one's attitude to the activity. Gardening and odd-job work around the home can be a chore or an absorbing hobby, and playing with the children can be a duty or a delight.

5 *Leisure, free time, spare time, uncommitted time, discretionary time, choosing time.* All the terms after "leisure" describe some aspect of what is meant by leisure.

We saw earlier that residual definitions of leisure give it as time free from various commitments and obligations, and that "free" time is best regarded as a dimension of leisure. "Spare" time is a slightly different idea, implying that, like a spare tire, it is not normally in use but could be put to use. "Uncommitted" time suggests a lack of obligations, of either a work or non-work character. "Discretionary" or "choosing" time is perhaps the essence of leisure, because it means time that we can use at our own discretion and according to our own choice.

By and large, serious leisure is found in the fifth category, although its occasional obligatory quality means that it sometimes falls into the fourth as well. It is obvious that the three types of serious leisure – amateurism, hobbyist pursuits, and volunteering – do not constitute work for most of those people engaged in them. That they are leisure, according to Parker's classification, is possibly less obvious.

I wish to begin by comparing these three types with the seven "essential elements of leisure" set out by Kaplan (1960, 22–5). These elements include: "a) an antithesis to "work" as an economic function; b) a pleasant expectation and recollection; c) a minimum of involuntary social-role obligations; d) a psychological perception of freedom; e) a close relation to values of the culture; f) an inclusion of an entire range from inconsequence and insignificance to weightiness and importance; and g) often, but not necessarily, an activity characterized by the element of play." These elements mesh with the subjective principle undergirding the conceptualization of leisure being developed here, namely, that leisure is actively defined as such by those engaging in it. Shaw's (1985) study of the definitions of leisure situations provides empirical support for this subjective approach.

Although amateurs and volunteers are sometimes paid for their efforts or expenses, or both (on volunteers, see Carter 1975, 92–5), these types of leisure hardly constitute a main source of income. Indeed, it is characteristic of serious leisure that its practitioners depend very little on whatever remuneration they derive from it. Moreover, whereas amateurs, hobbyists, and volunteers frequently incur obligations, and important ones at that, they are freer than breadwinners to renounce their leisure altogether (when particular obligations are not pressing for immediate fulfilment). Nonetheless, serious leisure enthusiasts are usually more obliged to engage in their pursuits than are their less serious counterparts. Like those counterparts, however, their overall impression of their involvement is a pleasant one. For the amateurs and volunteers, and for a small number of hobbyists, this positive view rests on the contribution their activity makes to their own well-being and to the life of the community. It follows that the element of play is rarely found in serious leisure.

During the current exploratory stage of research on serious leisure, seriousness is most effectively examined as a dichotomous quality, with casual or unserious leisure as its opposite.[2] Nonetheless, evidence from the Project indicates that seriousness and casualness among amateurs, as personal approaches to leisure, are merely the poles of a complicated dimension along which individuals may be ranked by their degrees of involvement in a particular activity. Hence, a more sophisticated, research-informed conception will eventually replace this primitive dichotomy. That conception will necessarily convey continuousness.

Turning now to the nature of serious leisure itself, I have so far identified six qualities that, taken together, distinguish it from casual leisure. One such quality is the occasional need to *persevere*. Despite participants' generally pleasant memory of such activity, there are moments when they suffer stage fright (Stebbins 1981), embarrassment (in stand-up comedy; in volunteer work, Floro 1978, 198), freezing cold (in astronomy), anxiety (in sport; in collecting, Dannefer 1980, 396), physical danger (in collecting, Fine 1988, 181; in hang-gliding, Brannigan and McDougall 1987), fatigue and injury (in baseball; football; running, Thompson, Stern, et al. 1979, Herskowitz 1972), and other strains. Indeed, Lewis (1982) describes ways in which business leaders "work at their leisure" as an extension of their work as executives. Nevertheless, it is clear that the positive feelings about the activity come, to some extent, from sticking with it through thick and thin, from conquering adversity.

A second quality of serious leisure is the tendency for amateurs, hobbyists, and volunteers to have *careers* in their endeavours. These endeavours are enduring pursuits with their own background contingencies, histories of turning points, and stages of achievement or involvement. They are anything but evanescent occurrences, devoid of social or psychological continuity. The volunteer, for instance, might return several days a week for many years to counsel delinquent girls; the amateur might paint and sell a dozen canvases in the span of a decade; the hobbyist runner (Nash 1979, 213–5) might recognize a progressive improvement in conditioning while training for future races.

Careers in serious leisure frequently rest on a third quality: significant personal *effort* based on specially acquired *knowledge, training,* or *skill,* and, indeed, sometimes all three. As the studies in the Project demonstrate, such characteristics as showmanship, athletic prowess, manual dexterity, scientific knowledge, verbal skills, long experience in a role, and, above all, persistent individual effort, differentiate amateurs and hobbyists from dabblers and the public at large, and volunteers from trainees and clients. Moreover, much, sometimes all, of this skill and knowledge is acquired outside formal education programs; it comes through self-directed learning (Carpenter, Patterson, et al. 1991).

Fourth, my research has turned up eight *durable benefits* found by amateurs in their various pursuits: self-actualization, self-enrichment, self-expression, recreation or renewal of self, feelings of accomplishment, enhancement of self-image, social interaction and belongingness, and lasting physical products of the activity. Only the ninth benefit – self-gratification or pure fun, which is considerably more evanescent than the preceding eight – also characterizes casual leisure. Self-gratification and, to a lesser extent, social interaction are usually the sole benefits accruing to partakers of the casual type. There is reason to believe that a systematic study of hobbyists and volunteers would result in similar listings of benefits or rewards, with lasting physical products being the least prevalent among the volunteers (see Altheide and Pfuhl 1980; Mitchell 1983, 137–69; Williams and Donnelly 1985; Irwin 1977; Neulinger 1981, 73).

A fifth quality differentiating serious from unserious leisure is the *unique ethos* that grows up around each instance of the former. Because of the previously mentioned qualities, amateurs, hobbyists, and volunteers tend to develop broad subcultures that are manifested in distinct ways in the "idiocultures" (Fine 1979) of a local group's special beliefs, norms, events, values, traditions, moral principles, and performance standards. Put another way, serious leisure participants carry on their interests within their own social worlds, worlds described as "amorphous, diffuse constellations of actors, organizations, events, and practices which have coalesced into spheres of interest and involvement for participants [and in which] it is likely that a powerful centralized authority structure does not exist" (Unruh 1980, 277). Much of casual leisure cannot be conceived of in these terms.

The sixth quality turns on the preceding five: participants in serious leisure tend to *identify* strongly with their chosen pursuits. They are inclined to speak proudly, excitedly, and frequently about them to other people, and to present themselves in terms of these pursuits when conversing with new acquaintances. Research on amateurs indicates that they often realize they are sometimes too enthusiastic in discussions about their avocations. In contrast, unserious leisure, though hardly humiliating or despicable, is nonetheless too fleeting, mundane, and commonplace for most people to find a distinctive identity within it.

It should be clear from the contents of this section that the adjective "serious" embodies such qualities as earnestness, sincerity, importance, and carefulness, rather than gravity, solemnity, joylessness, distress, and anxiety. Although the terms in the second list occasionally describe serious leisure events, they are uncharacteristic of them and fail to nullify, or, in many cases, even dilute, the overall pleasure gained by the participants.

The foregoing discussion also indicates that serious leisure is just as often described and analyzed in terms appropriate to the world of work as in those appropriate to the world of leisure. It seems, then, that hobbyists and volunteers can be classed with amateurs as marginal men and women of leisure (see chapter 3).

MODERN AMATEURISM

As professionalization spreads from one occupation to another, what was once considered play in some of these spheres is evolving quietly, inevitably, and unnoticeably into a new form – one best named *modern amateurism*. Modern amateurism has been evolving alongside those occupations where some of the participants in the occupation are now able to make a substantial living from it and, consequently, to devote themselves to it as a vocation rather than an avocation. Although there are possibly others, we can label science, entertainment, sport and games, as well as fine arts, as the major occupational areas where work was once purely play and where modern amateurism is now a parallel development.

What has been happening is that those who play at the activities encompassed by these occupations are being overrun in significance, if not in numbers, by professionals and amateurs. It is a process that seems to unfold as follows. As opportunities for full-time pursuit of a skill or activity gradually appear, those people with even an average aptitude for such skills are able to develop them to a level observably higher than that of the typical part-time participant. With today's mass availability of professional performances (or products), whatever the field, new standards of excellence soon confront all participants, professional or not. Although the performances of the professionals are frequently impressive, no category of participant is more impressed than that of the non-professionals who, through direct experience, know the activity intimately. Indeed, once they become aware of the professional standards, all they have accomplished seems mediocre by comparison. They are thus faced with a critical choice in their careers as participants: either they restrict identification with the activity so as to remain largely unaffected by such invidious comparisons, or they identify sufficiently with it to attempt to meet those standards.

With the first choice, which is still common, the part-time participant remains a player, dabbler, or dilettante. Following Huizinga's (1955) perspective on play, we can say that leisure of that type lacks necessity, obligation, and utility and will be produced with a disinterestedness that sets it, as an activity, apart from the participants' ordinary, real lives. The second choice, also common and becoming more so, impels part-time participants away from play toward the pursuit of durable benefits. The road to these benefits, however, is characterized by necessity, obligation, seriousness, and commitment, as expressed by regimentation (e.g., rehearsals and practice) and systematization (e.g., schedules and organization), and progresses on to the status of modern amateur for some and professional for others. Godbout (1986) has noted this trend in what he calls the "professionalization of leisure" (also known as regimentation or systematization).

The player of old in sport and music, and quite possibly other fields, was referred to as a "gentleman" (very few were women). But first Huizinga (1955, ch. 12), and then Stone (1972, 48), have commented on such players gradual disappearance from sport. Indeed, it is an ongoing process. Barzun (1956b, 61) points to this transformation in music.

There was a time, furthermore, when players and amateurs (probably differences existed between them even then) were alone in their activities – without professionals to compete against, model themselves after, or simply mingle with. In fact, the early history of many contemporary professions was made up exclusively of amateurs, the only people practising the professions in their day. In effect, these endeavours were too new, too little in demand, or too underdeveloped to be pursued as livelihoods. In other words, when their fields began, a number of astronomers, archaeologists, teachers, musicians, painters, jugglers, bowlers, soccer players, and so forth earned their living doing something else; clearly, however, they were experts, by the standards of the day, in their respective areas of leisure.

In some fields amateurism was an honourable tradition, and attempts at full-time employment, to say nothing of professionalization, were actually met with derision. At the time, it was considered despicable to make money in this way. But, as the two categories of participant began to diverge, it remains to be discovered just how many fields existed in which amateurs could be distinguished from professionals by social class. Whannel (1983, 43) notes that, in the nineteenth century, those who played sport for money belonged to the lower class, whereas those who played purely for enjoyment belonged to the upper class. For many years, informal, sometimes even formal, arrangements prevented the different classes of teams and individuals from competing with one another.

As professionals begin to dominate a field pioneered by amateurs, however, a transformation in the meaning of "amateur" seems to have occurred. During this period, old definitions clung tenaciously, merging in common discourse with the new ones springing up to describe modern amateurism. From a research standpoint, the result was the emergence of the idea of amateur, a term which is now used with an annoying imprecision in everyday life. The entries in *Webster's Unabridged Dictionary* exemplify the problem. Amateurs, for instance, are defined, in one sense, as devotees who love a particular activity; in another sense, however, they are considered superficial participants – dilettantes or dabblers. Dilettantes, on the other hand, are defined, in the first sense, as lovers of the arts and, in the second, as people with discrimination or taste. Consider, also, the logical difficulties posed by yet another sense of "amateur" – that is, the inexperienced person (or player) – and the patent fact that devotees of an activity quite naturally put in much time at it, thereby achieving remarkable competence (i.e., modern amateurs).

When I happened onto the study of amateurism in the early 1970s, sociology was also beset by more or less the same confusion of definitions. Because the matter is still sufficiently complicated to require separate and extensive treatment (see chapters 2 and 3), I have focused in this chapter on the discussion of two brief definitions, thereby avoiding any digression from the central subject of serious leisure. One definition is macrosociological in intent: amateurs are considered to be members of a professional-amateur-public (PAP) system of relations and relationships. The other is microsociological, or social psychological: amateurs hold certain attitudes that differentiate them from both professionals and their publics.

HOBBYIST PURSUITS

Both hobbyists and amateurs are practitioners in definite and lasting pursuits. Hobbyists are serious about and committed to their endeavours, even though they feel neither a social necessity nor a personal obligation to engage in them. In other words, they are not dabblers aimlessly doing something as a temporary diversion. A hobby is a specialized pursuit beyond one's occupation, a pursuit that one finds particularly interesting and enjoyable because of its durable benefits.

A crucial difference between hobbyists and amateurs is that the hobbyists are not part of any PAP system. Although uncommon, hobbyists may have a commercial public, for example the part-time toy makers who sell to a local market. A commercial equivalent may also exist, such as fishing-equipment manufacturers for hobbyist fly-tiers. But those commercial equivalents differ significantly from members of a "profession," as this term is usually understood. Indeed, hobbyists are often enamoured of pursuits bearing little or no resemblance to ordinary work roles. As for publics in general, they seem to be as prevalent and important for hobbyists, as a category, as for amateurs. In other words we can speak of a hobbyist-public (HP) system.

Any monetary interests in a hobby are secondary, when compared with its other durable benefits. The studies of hobbyists cited throughout this section support this proposition, in the sense that remuneration is never mentioned as a reason for engaging in the activities. In other words, neither hobbies nor amateur pursuits are entered into primarily as a way to supplement the practitioner's main income. They are not "second jobs." In effect, there is a certain devotion attached to these forms of serious leisure that suggests they would be practised whether a financial gain or loss resulted. Indeed, if a substantial amount of money is earned during their pursuit, that is but one reward of many and, according to evidence at hand, one of the least significant. Many "sideline" businesses, including some so-called "hobby farms," are thus excluded from consideration as true hobbies.

Hobbyists fall into four categories. One is the *collector* of, for instance, stamps, rare books, butterflies, violins, minerals, or paintings. It is the collector who develops a technical knowledge of the commercial, social, and physical circumstances in which the desired items are acquired.[3] These collectors also develop a sophisticated appreciation of these items, along with a broad understanding of their historical and contemporary production and use. This knowledge, appreciation, and understanding is illustrated in Dannefer's (1980) ethnography of the social world of the old-car collector; in Christ's (1965), Olmsted's (1987) and Gelber's (in press) studies of stamp collectors; and in Olmsted and Horna's (1989) study of pin collectors. Olmsted (1988) also examines the technical knowledge and skills, as well as the appropriate attitudes, needed for admission into a Canadian gun and cartridge collectors' association.

Hobbyist collectors are distinguishable from commercial dealers. Dealers acquire their stock to make a living by subsequent sales; the motive is completely different from that which drives hobbyist collectors. Although the latter may try to make money by selling a violin or painting in order to buy one that is more valuable, they are usually interested in gaining a prestigious item for personal and social reasons, or possibly for hedging inflation, rather than in earning a livelihood.

The casual collecting of such things as matchbooks, beer bottles, or travel pennants is, at best, a marginal instance of "hobbyism" (to coin a word). Here, there is no equivalent complex of commercial, social, and physical circumstances about which to learn; no substantial aesthetic or technical appreciation possible; no comparable level of understanding as to production and use to be developed. Casual collecting is thus most accurately classified under casual leisure, as a pastime.

Makers and tinkerers comprise the second group of hobbyists. Here is the conceptual home of such enthusiasts as inventors, flytiers, seamstresses, furniture and toy makers, automobile repairers, boat builders, knitters and weavers, quilters (Cooper and Buferd 1977), lapidary workers, indoor gardeners, home remodellers (where this is a recurrent activity), model airplane builders (Butsch 1984), and handicrafters (where no professional counterpart exists). Mind you, the do-it-yourself drudge who paints the exterior of his or her house to avoid the expense of a full-time tradesperson is not an example of the hobbyist home remodeller. Nor can we regard the branches of commercial automobile repair, clothing manufacture, and pottery making as instances of the category of leisure making or tinkering.

Although it may seem somewhat curious, the inclusion of those who avocationally breed or display animals, birds, reptiles, and fish is consistent with the underlying logic of this "maker" category. A study by Floro (1983) on breeding dairy goats and a brief ethnographic discussion of aquarists, or those who breed or display tropical fish, by Bishop and Hodgett (1986), demonstrate the validity of this taxonomic decision. Under this same heading would fall those people who breed or display as an avocation such animals as dogs, cats, sheep, horses, ferrets, and, as was done recently in the mountainous areas of western North America, llamas.

The third kind of hobbyist is the *activity participant*. Such people steadfastly pursue a form of leisure requiring systematic physical movement that has intrinsic appeal and is conducted within a set of rules. Often the activity poses a challenge, albeit a noncompetitive one. When carried out continually and purposely for these reasons, the following activities can be included within that category: fishing (Bryan 1977; Graefe and Fedler 1985); bird-watching (Kellert 1985); mountaineering (Slovenko and Knight 1967; Mitchell 1983; Williams and Donnelly 1985; Ewert 1985); deer hunting (Hautaluoma and Brown 1978); morris dancing (Bishop and Hodgett 1986); hang-gliding (Brannigan and McDougall 1987); body-building (Klein 1985; Duff and Hong 1984; Bednarek 1985); barbershop singing (Stebbins 1992); sailing (Macbeth 1988); wave surfing (Irwin 1977; Pearson 1980; Kamphorst and Giljam 1984); alpine skiing (Irwin 1977; Slovenko and Knight 1967);

playing video games (Selnow 1987; Toles 1985; Ng and June 1985; Podilchak 1986); and participating in gymnastics (Slovenko and Knight 1967). The works referred to present informative ethnographic, and sometimes social psychological and sociological data as well, on an activity. Bryan (1979) offers much briefer but, nonetheless, scientifically useful treatments of canoeing and backpacking.

The *folk artist* is a type of activity participant as well. Since the PAP system is based on a certain degree of social interaction among members of the three groups, non-professional practitioners who, as a group, have little or no interchange with professionals or amateurs are logically excluded from the category of modern amateur. Lacking a more suitable term, for there appears to be no equivalent outside the arts, these enthusiasts are referred to here as folk artists. They are not to be confused with commercial performers or producers of these arts. Rather, they perform or produce strictly for their own enjoyment and perhaps that of others in the same community, while making their living in some other fashion. They know little about professional standards of music, craft, art, or theatre, although they may unwittingly meet some of them. Having no contact with a particular PAP system, they contribute nothing, as a rule, to any of its component groups, including the public. Certain folk artists in art, music, and theatre are treated in greater detail by Becker (1982, 246–58), Ramsey (1970), Thurston (1988), and Halpert and Story (1969).

When their pursuits are competitive, hobbyists can be classified in a fourth way: as *players* of sports or games or in competitions associated with some of the activities mentioned in the preceding category (e.g., body-building, barbershop singing). Like those in the preceding category, players relate to each other according to a set of rules that structure their actions during a contest. Here we find softball (Glancy 1986); table shuffleboard (Senters 1971); target shooting (Hummel 1985); field hockey (Bishop and Hodgett 1986); badminton and outdoor bowls (Boothby and Tungatt 1978); dirt-bike racing (Watson, Legg et al. 1980); long-distance running (Yair 1990; Barrel et al. 1989); role-playing games (Fine 1983); survival games (Reeves 1986); martial arts (James and Jones 1982); competitive mountaineering (Hamilton 1979); swimming (Hastings 1983; Hastings, Kurth, et al. 1989); parachuting (Aran 1974); fencing, and track and field (Slovenko and Knight 1967). Still to be studied ethnographically are such sports and games as darts, volleyball, orienteering, rowing, and computer games.

What the hobbyists in this category have in common is the lack of a true professional counterpart. Consistent with the definition of a "hobbyist," their participation is continual and systematic. The aim is to acquire and maintain the knowledge and skills enabling the individual to experience uncommon rewards from the endeavour. Still, this orientation, whatever the type of serious leisure, can have unwanted consequences, as the following observations apropos dedicated runners suggest: "Direct conflict between the runner and his or her spouse or partner over such issues as neglect, loss of shared interests, friends, fatigue, and neglect of work was found to be consistently related to commitment to running. Higher levels of time and intensity commitment, subcultural involvement, and cognitive identification are associated with more intense complaints of the runner by his or her partner" (Robbins and Joseph 1980, 97–8).

Such sports and games as baseball, hockey, rugby, chess, and recently shuffleboard (Snyder 1986) are more accurately placed under the heading of amateurism, owing to their location in the PAP system. Other sports, such as racketball (Adler and Adler 1982; Spreitzer and Snyder 1983) and possibly bicycle racing (Albert 1984, 331; Wayne 1990) and darts, now that they are in the process of becoming professionalized, are impossible to classify at present.

Because duplicate bridge is pursued by "players" who lack true professional counterparts, it is termed a hobby. Holtz (1975), however, writes that "professional" duplicate bridge players are really quasi-deviant hustlers working as secretly paid partners in a leisure activity that is officially held to be strictly amateur. Thus the so-called professionals in bridge, at least from what we know about them so far, fail to conform to the sociological definitions of a professional (see next chapter), a litmus test that happily removes professional criminals (Klein 1974) from consideration in this regard.

Some hobbyists fit more than one category, such as the builders of motorized model airplanes who ultimately fly their constructions in a nearby field. The classification of individual hobbyists also depends partly on the context in which they pursue their activities. For example, swimmer number one is termed a player because he competes in swimming meets. Swimmer number two, however, is termed an activity participant, because she swims for the pleasure of the development and maintenance of her skill, as well as for the exercise it provides.

Several hobbies in the arts, science, sport, and entertainment areas have evolved over the years into full-time livelihoods and, ultimately, into professions. As professionalization occurs, those who retain their serious, albeit part-time, commitment to the activity are gradually transformed into amateurs. Before this, in the early days of the activity, all participants were so-called gentlemen amateurs, usually independently wealthy individuals who had time to devote to leisure interests. In other words, the emerging professionalism is paralleled by an emerging amateurism. Through the PAP system that is taking shape, the amateurs learn what full-time work at their hobby can produce; depending on the area, that can mean greater rates of productivity, increased complexity of knowledge and instrumentation, new standards of performance excellence, expanded and formalized training requirements, and so on. Eventually, the part-time pursuit of the activity is reshaped, in the sense that, increasingly, it is modeled after its new professional counterpart. Historical research by Ainley (1980) and Lankford (1981a; 1981b) describe how this transformation unfolded in ornithology and astronomy, respectively. I have presented similar histories in my books on magic, stand-up comedy, and Canadian football.[4]

CAREER VOLUNTEERING

Van Til (1988, 5–9) outlines the essential differences between voluntary action and its subcategory of interest, namely, volunteering, to us as follows: voluntary action is individual action that is uncoerced and not primarily aimed toward financial gain, whereas volunteering is individual or group action that is voluntary and oriented toward helping others or oneself. Bosserman and Gagan (1972, 115) and Smith (1975, 148) hold that, at the individual level, all leisure activity is voluntary action. In fact, such action is occasionally found in non-leisure activities. Voluntary action (and therefore volunteering) is never undertaken for such compelling reasons as economic benefit, self-preservation, physical coercion, physiological need, or psychic or social compulsion. Its component of serving others, however, has been shown (Neulinger 1981, 19) to be an important leisure pursuit. And, to repeat a point made earlier, we must remain especially attuned, in this area, to the possibility of participants defining volunteering as work, as do some retirees and those who volunteer as preparation for a work career (see Jenner 1982).

Clearly, according to the conceptual scheme used by Statistics Canada (1980), the scope of career volunteering is extremely broad. It touches seven types of organizations, within which different services are provided: health (physical and non-physical health care for all ages), educational (service inside and outside the formal school system), social/welfare (child care, family counselling, correctional services), leisure (service in athletic and nonathletic associations), religious (service in religious associations), civic/community action (advocacy, service in professional and labour organizations), and political (service in political organizations). Managerial, clerical, stenographic, and advisory services are among the other ones provided.[5]

Because volunteering, when viewed as a type of serious leisure, is a recurring skill- and knowledge-based activity which can provide people with a career in a special social world, the other two categories frequently studied as voluntary action – financial help and gifts of self – are excluded from the present discussion.[6] Donations of clothing and money, for instance, may be recurrent, but they hardly meet the other criteria of volunteering as serious leisure. Indeed, the giving of gifts – eyes, blood, organs, tissues, furniture, and so forth (normally one-shot contributions, except for furniture) – is pleasant only in terms of the altruistic feelings generated by one's magnanimity.

Two aspects of the volunteering role distinguish its incumbents from the first two types of serious leisure participants. One of these is *altruism*. Although it is now established that volunteers are usually driven by both altruistic and self-interested motives (National Advisory Council on Voluntary Action 1978; 11; Carter 1975, 83; Alberta Recreation and Parks 1990; Henderson 1981, 213), altruism influences volunteers far more than it influences amateurs and hobbyists.

The second aspect involves the *delegated tasks* volunteers typically perform, tasks offered them by their superiors who are employed in the organization in which the volunteers serve.[7] These tasks are ones that the professional or managerial staff of the organization believe the volunteers can do, given adequate training and experience, and that staff believe are beyond their jurisdiction or, given budgetary limitations, cannot do themselves. This turns volunteers into "outsiders" in work organizations or agencies otherwise composed of insiders (Floro 1978, 198). Indeed, they may even be threatening to some of the insiders (Deegan and Nutt 1975, 351; Joyce Williams 1987). It is for these reasons that volunteers usually require sponsors (Floro 1978, 197), an arrangement unheard of in the individualized forms of amateurism and hobbyism. In their collective forms, try-outs provide sufficient and immediate proof of a performer's or an athlete's excellence, obviating the need for a sponsor. All this means that volunteers are neither facsimiles of professionals, as amateurs are, nor bureaucratized workers. Rather, they are, most commonly, a special class of helper in someone else's occupational world (Floro 1978, 194).[8]

These two aspects enable volunteers, as they pursue their serious leisure, to contribute to society in a unique way. This they do by *helping*. That helping contrasts with the contributions of amateurs and hobbyists, whose commercial, scientific, sport, artistic, and entertainment activities are fundamentally *cultural*. While amateurs and hobbyists do help on occasion, as in the case of the avocational scientists who collect data for professional analysts, helping is only a secondary goal; it is but a collateral consequence of their self-interested search for leisure with durable benefit. As already mentioned, there may be considerable self-sacrifice involved, but personal reasons are the prime motivator, with altruism in second place.

In their pursuit of serious leisure, volunteers come close to balancing these values. Although they gain durable personal benefits from their endeavours, helping remains an important aim. When amateurs and hobbyists persevere at the difficult requirements of their leisure, they do so because they are devoted and because hard work engenders feelings of accomplishment. When volunteers persevere, however, they do so with the conviction that they are needed; to weaken in the face of adversity is to let down others, disappoint them, or leave serious personal or social problems unresolved. Nonetheless, Parker's (1987a) research on British and Australian volunteers indicates that they very much enjoy this form of leisure. Personal satisfaction is part of the reward as well.

Volunteers and amateurs do, however, make one similar contribution; in their own way they relate the occupation or organization with which they are associated to its public or clients. Lauffer and Gorodezky (1977, 10) have noted, for example, that "volunteers sometimes speak the clients' language more directly than paid staff." The Project demonstrates that in science, for instance, amateurs are recognized for their public relations efforts, as when they work to educate the citizenry in the fundamentals of the discipline or to lobby the government for favourable legislation (see also Mayfield 1979, 169).

But what empirical evidence do we have to support this idea of career volunteering as a type of serious leisure? At the moment very little, if one looks for studies directly linking these two concepts. Indeed, Henderson (1981) notes that research linking volunteering and leisure is, in general, rare. To my knowledge, Parker's (1987a; 1987b) two papers stand alone as the sole studies of serious leisure and volunteering. Floro (1990) also joined the two concepts in a review essay of Richard Bach's *Gift of Wings*. Nonetheless, the number of studies that deal with the voluntary action perspective of career volunteers, as well as volunteering in the seven types of organizations noted earlier, is voluminous. They are abstracted regularly in *Voluntarism Review and Reporter*.

CONCLUSIONS

Table 1 summarizes the conceptual discussion of the previous three sections. Lest there be any confusion, I have used the term "differentiating principle" to mean the general process (motivation, contribution) or structure (institutional role) that distinguishes amateurs, hobbyists,

Table 1
Distinctive Attributes of the Types of Serious Leisure*

Differentiating principle	Amateurism	Hobbyism	Volunteering
Motivation	1 Self-interest 2 Public interest 3 Altruism 4 Pecuniary interest	1 Self-interest 2 Public interest 3 Pecuniary interest	1 Altruism; Self-interest
Institutional role	1 Near professional	1 Non-work	1 Delegated work
Contribution	1 Satisfaction 2 Cultural 3 Helping 4 Commercial	1 Satisfaction 2 Cultural 3 Commercial	1 Helping; Satisfaction

* The higher the number, the more central is the attribute to the type of serious leisure.

and volunteers one from another. The number preceding each attribute signifies its rank order in terms of the degree of significance ascribed to it by the typical participant. The higher the number, the less significant is the attribute. Indeed, depending on the type of serious leisure under consideration, the second, third, and fourth attributes apply only to a minority of individual participants. This ranking is based on current knowledge about the three types. Since research in this area is badly needed, new data could well change this pattern, perhaps dramatically.

But the case for considering serious leisure does not end with a call to social science researchers to give it more attention. For at least some people, it offers an attractive alternative to the typical job, and in an age when jobs are consuming less and less of our time yet still functioning as the main source of personal income. Yet, as Roberts (1981, 61) says, people must either discover for themselves, or be shown, that "leisure is not always a good time. Freedom to choose never guarantees happiness." According to Roberts, the growth of leisure does not automatically enhance the quality of life; it merely bestows the opportunity for such enhancement, thereby underlining the urgency of helping people find ways of deriving the maximum benefit from their scope for choice, and forcing enquiry into why leisure sometimes fails to deliver the promised fulfilment.

I believe that implicit in Roberts' statements is the suggestion that a steady diet of casual, unserious leisure in the sizable blocks of time left over after a substantially reduced workweek, month, or year, ultimately tends to cause a spiritual wasteland. What is needed is the encouragement and opportunity to participate in serious leisure, backed by the sort of education that makes this possible. This is, in fact, the conclusion reached in the final chapter of this book. The logical and empirical support for this recommendation is contained in the intervening chapters on amateurs and professionals. Let us turn first to the professionals.

CHAPTER TWO

Professionals

Although this chapter is chiefly about professionals, I begin by comparing them with amateurs. Frequently, our everyday English usage of the term "amateur," and related words, invokes direct or indirect reference to the term "professional," and its related words. Indeed, this appears to be a central theme, which can provide a starting point for a sociological definition. *Webster's Dictionary* defines amateur in one sense as "one that engages in a particular pursuit, study, or science as a pastime rather than as a professional." In the same dictionary "amateurism" is defined as "non-professional," and "amateurish" as the lack of a professional finish. For a fuller understanding of the idea, readers are invited to compare the "amateurism" entry with that of the "professional." Incidentally, the latter entry urges comparison with the former.[1] Turning to everyday life, the reference to professional was found to be a central defining point throughout this Project.

Among the amateurs and professionals I observed and interviewed, I found the same tendency as in the larger community: they differentiated the two categories in one or two oversimplified ways. First, they spoke of professionals as gaining at least 50 percent of their livelihood from their pursuit, and of amateurs as, at the most, only supplementing a principal source of income earned elsewhere. Second, they spoke of professionals as spending considerably more time at their pursuits than do amateurs. Although we could build a scientific definition from either of these two truisms that would distinguish one from the other, we would have gained little useful knowledge. In the end, such unidimensional definitions fail to communicate the essence of either status. Indeed, I encountered scores of devoted amateurs in all four areas who spend at least as much time at their serious leisure as they do at their occupations. Incidentally, that *is* humanly possible.[2] A further disadvantage of these two common sense definitions is that they have never found their way into sociological theory.

The two brief definitions of amateur presented in the preceding chapter, developed at the beginning of the Project, were used to guide research from there on. Although these definitions avoid the aforementioned weaknesses, the macrosociological version, which defined amateur as part of a professional-amateur-public (PAP) system of relations and relationships, had to undergo several important modifications. First, I came to realize that the earlier version of "functionally interdependent relationships" was erroneous and simplistic. For instance, although the relations and relationships can, indeed, be functional, they may also be dysfunctional. Moreover, at times they conflict and, at other times, they are harmonious. The complexity of this system can be seen in the discussion found in chapters 3 through 7.

In the present chapter, I examine the professional component of the PAP system. The amateur and public components are taken up in chapters 3 and 4. If the tone of the discussion in this chapter seems polemical, it is because the attributional definition championed here is controversial. Indeed, my broadest goal is to argue for its utility, based on what was learned about public-centred professionals during the course of the Project.

THE COMMON SENSE VIEW OF
PROFESSIONAL

The modern common sense and scientific conceptions of the professional are two starkly contrasting understandings of one of the most prestigious forms of work in modern times. As earlier discussion suggests, the common sense conception tends to be *quantitative* and *empirical*. Briefly, it is the following: professionals are seen by the average person and, as noted, by many professionals and amateurs, as people who spend the majority of their working hours enacting their professional roles, roles from which they receive the bulk of their livelihood, based upon the excellence of their service rendered in this capacity. The amounts of time spent and money made while on the professional job, as well as the excellence of the service provided, are measurable aspects of this type of work.

From the standpoint of common sense, the measurability of the excellence of service provided refers to the "better than" quality of certain categories of professionals, particularly those in the arts, sciences, sports, and entertainment fields. Here the general public makes comparisons, usually in an off-hand way, with a set of adult amateurs. Thus the professionals in these fields are believed to be "better than" their amateur counterparts, as measured by, for example, better pitching of a baseball, better performance of a concerto, or better design of a research project.

But there are professions in which there are no true amateurs, professions in which the common sense viewpoint must, of necessity, centre on measurable criteria other than that "better than" criterion. Professionals in this category serve individual clients, as can be seen in the work of nurses, lawyers, physicians, schoolteachers, social workers, and others whose professional qualifications are determined by examination and state-run licensing procedures. One becomes a professional in these fields by passing the appropriate test and receiving a lawful licence to practise. Hence, here, the common sense criterion of excellence is met by the measurable career turning point of "passing the boards." But inasmuch as amateurs do the same things for leisure that professionals do for a living (see chapter 3) and are legally prevented from participating in these fields, they are, by the same token, effectively eliminated from any such comparisons there.

In line with the goal just mentioned, I shall compare this common sense conception of the professional with two very different conceptions held by sociologists. In addition, I shall try to show how one of these conceptions can be elaborated, using exploratory research data on *public-centred* professions in art, science, sport, and entertainment, almost all of which comes from the Project.[3] Here publics consume a professional *production* or *work*, such as a game, show, concert, exhibition, or scientific study, rather than a professional *service*, such as advice, diagnosis, counselling, treatment, representation, or registration, typical contributions of the client-centred professions. I am aware of only one area of overlap between these two types of professions: namely, the client orientation of public-centred professionals who work by commission (in architecture, see Blau 1987, 8–9).

SOCIOLOGICAL VIEWS OF
PROFESSIONALS

The two sociological conceptions tend to be *qualitative* and *theoretical*. The first of these to appear was the *attribution approach*, the components of which are variously referred to as traits, attributes, or characteristics and often presented in ideal-typical terms. Throughout this book, I will focus strictly on the attributions and will consider them independently of the functionalist theory sometimes associated with them. The second conception, which arose in response to certain weaknesses of the first, will be presented later under the heading of *power and professions*.

Starting with Ernest Greenwood (1957), the work of a number of sociologists, among them Parsons (1968, 536), Gross (1958, 77–82), and Kaplan (1960, 203–4), led to the development of a list of attributes describing the "professionalism" of those occupations commonly referred to as professions. Except when incorporated into functionalist theory, these attributes amounted to little more than separate, and often unrelated, elements of a developing sociological definition of a profession. Nine attributes can be abstracted from this literature, to which I will add a tenth later on. The first nine are presented here in ideal-typical terms and include several elaborations suggested by my own research on public-centred professionals, as well as that of others.

1 Professionals turn out unstandardized products and services.
2 Professionals are well versed in an exclusive body of theoretical knowledge and, at times, technique.
3 Professionals share a strong sense of identity with their colleagues, from whom they develop a sense of community, a sense of being members of an in-group.
4 Professionals master a generalized cultural tradition associated with their line of work.
5 Professionals use institutionalized means of formally or consensually validating the adequacy of training and the competency of trained individuals.
6 Professional work constitutes a calling in which the primary concerns are consistent application of a standard and provision of a service or product, and the actual monetary return is secondary to the work itself.
7 Professionals are recognized by their clients or publics for their special authority, based on knowledge, experience, and, in some cases, technique.
8 Professional services and products provide an avenue for attainment of certain important social values.
9 Professional work is self-regulated or autonomous.

The attribution approach to defining and understanding professions has its critics. Hall (1986, 44), citing Roth's (1974) critique, argues not only that this approach is now *passée* but that the attempts to develop a similar, but more refined model, have largely been abandoned. Roth, himself, believes that lists of attributes "are largely mixtures of unproved – indeed, unexamined – claims for professional control and autonomy" (Roth 1974, 7). Moreover, he characterizes as "deadend" Greenwood's (1957) suggestion that the various occupations fall along a continuum, at one end of which lies a key attribute of the profession in question. What is worse, says Roth, is that such an undertaking deflects attention from the history of an occupation and its process of professionalization, as well as from the power that professions have developed over time to manipulate society in their own interests (see also Hall 1986, 44–55).

Roth's critique, however, is wide of the mark on a number of counts. First, the attribution approach, freed of its functionalist bias, is basically an attempt to define the idea of a professional. When we define something we attempt to identify its essential nature, its key attributes. Roth and Hall, among others, would thus seem to be rejecting attempts at definition. Moreover, even if it were possible, it would certainly be reckless to write about professionals without a scientific definition, particularly in an age when the common sense usage of the term is extremely loose and an erroneous, even simplistic, quantitative-empirical conception prevails. In Freidson's words: "Without *some* definition of profession, the concept of professionalization is virtually meaningless, as is the intention to study process rather than structure. One cannot study process without a definition to guide one's focus, any more fruitfully than one can study structure without a definition" (Freidson 1983a, 22). This explains my reluctance to jettison the attributions. Such a step is premature when they still offer, by means of descriptive, ideal-typical research, a solution to the problem of definition.

Talk of process leads us to a second weakness in the Hall/Roth critique. Roth urges study of the process of professionalization, deeming it more fruitful than the study of attributes. But processes beget products, in our case the cultural and structural attributes just mentioned. Certainly they are also worthy of study. Thus we are forced to return to the question of what that product is. In other words, we must still ask what a profession is and how we define it.

Third, as if it were proof that the attribution approach is unnecessary, Roth asserts that the attributes identified so far are unproved and sometimes even unexamined. Although that has been deplorably true in the past, it is hardly a reason to abandon all efforts to study these attributes empirically and arrive thereby at a valid definition of a profession. In this connection, Roth has provided data that refute some of the attributes.

Nonetheless, as noted at the beginning of this section, there is one problem with the attribution approach: its tendency to be qualitative and theoretical. Indeed, the attributes are generally unmeasurable quantitatively. They are, moreover, theoretical, since each is really a hypothetical proposition about the professions. So we must then ask ourselves whether professions actually have these attributes. How do their manifestations vary from one profession to another? Both Greenwood and Roth seem to agree that some, or all, of these attributes are found in other categories of occupations as well: for example, in management and the skilled trades. How, then, do these attributes vary from one occupational category to another? In short, definitions are propositions, or sets of propositions, that are to be tested, not simply assumed. Such testing has been extremely rare in this area.

We now have a textbook example of premature theoretical closure, instigated chiefly by the attribution theorists themselves, in which a set of definitional propositions has gained scientific acceptance as established fact even though the empirical scrutiny was minimal. One way out of the resulting conceptual confusion would be to treat the field as if it were still at the exploratory stage of research design and theoretical development. At this stage, the attributes are best treated – as I have tried to do here – as components of an ideal-typical definition of professional (Lopreato and Alston 1970). Incidentally, ideal-types do not necessarily correspond to empirical reality. Rather, they are exploratory models to be used in comparison with actual cases, so as to determine what variation, if any, exists between the pure type and reality. Certainly to present an ideal-type is not to assert its truth; that can only come from examining actual cases.

The variations observed may, in fact, be quantitative or qualitative, even some of both. For example, physicians might express their professional commitment (calling) not only by consulting extensively with specialists but by reading widely in the medical literature about the ailment of a patient, even though that patient will pay no more for the next office visit than the other patients whose ailments require less "homework." Or football players might express their professional commitment by sticking to an exceptionally rigorous training regimen. If such a regimen affects their salary, it will only be applicable to next year's contract, and within the context of an overall job evaluation by team management.

As far as public-centred professionals are concerned, the comparative studies of amateurs and professionals undertaken in the Project offer evidence as to the validity of the first nine attributes. That is, these attributes are evident among professionals in art, science, sport, and entertainment and, to a considerable degree, even among amateurs. Because these studies concentrated on public-centred rather than client-centred professionals, they also produced a number of elaborations to the nine ideal-typical attributes originally developed with reference to the latter. Indeed, the inductive analysis that accompanies my explorations, the methodological approach of this project, made these discoveries possible. We turn next to the elaborations.

ELABORATIONS

1 *Professionals turn out unstandardized products and services.* For professionals who work with clients, such a statement is obvious, inasmuch as the ideal professional *service* is, among other things, more or less tailored to individual needs and personalities. Indeed, it is a unique, or at best highly unusual, service. By comparison, professionals who serve publics offer unique *products*, to the extent that a painting, rendition of a concerto, scientific journal article, play in baseball, or performance by a magician can be termed a singular event. Mind you, succeeding events of the same type, involving the same people, are never exactly the same. While this reality is self-evident in art, science, and entertainment, perhaps it is less so in sport, although the following excerpt from the football study suggests that athletes, too, live up to this first attribute of the professional.

The product or performance produced by football players is always unique in some way. Every game is unique, as is the play of each player once the ball is snapped. No receiver, for example, has the ball thrown to him exactly the same way with each pass. Nor is he guarded by the defensive backs the same way from pass to pass. The receiver's field position is also different to some extent with each pass play he runs. In each play, every player on the field makes a set of unique, split-second decisions and reactions in response to the actions unfolding before him.

Thus the attribute of the unstandardized product can be elaborated beyond the standard conception. It does, however, require that professionals be seen as people who can serve publics or clients, and possibly both. Witness, for instance, the artist who is commissioned to paint a portrait.

2 *Professionals are well versed in an exclusive body of specialized theoretical knowledge and, at times, technique.* Professionals are highly trained experts in the application of relevant theory, or at least abstract principles, to the solution of difficult problems, often, but not always, by means of considerable physical skill. The theory or principles are so difficult and complex that special training and commitment are necessary to acquire them. Hence their exclusivity, although this exclusivity may also be assured by concerted attempts to limit or discourage access of certain ethnic, gender, or socioeconomic groups to such training. All this falls under the "principle of indeterminacy" (Jamous and Peloille 1970) – the unavailability of professional knowledge and technique to the laity.

The products and performances of professionals in art and science certainly indicate the presence of specialized knowledge and, at times, technique. This specialization is also evident in the sports and entertainment fields, although knowledge here is less often codified, as in books, and often subtly linked to accumulated *experience* gained from practising the sport or entertainment in question. Thus, professional comics were observed to apply many of the principles of theatre in their use of timing, eye contact, voice projection, verbal diction, physical gesture, vocal inflection, effective rhythm, and the like. And veteran football players, based on their knowledge of the usual offences and defences, developed an ability to "read" the plays of their opponents quickly.

The experience factor, by the way, is as important in the client-centred professions as in the public-centred ones. I found that, for entertainers, fine artists, and sports people in the eight studies of this Project, a major way of differentiating professionals from amateurs was to determine their experience in performing the role in question. It appears that in such professions as baseball and theatre, where theoretical knowledge is peripheral, experience is of much greater importance than in such professions as science and law, whether theoretical knowledge is central.

Critics of this attribute (e.g., Hall 1986, 42) point to the fact that some professions require more training than is needed for actual professional practice. Further, Roth (1974) says that the knowledge base is sometimes inconsistent when, as in medicine for instance, new theories replace old ones. But these observations are irrelevant. It is not the fact of being overtrained, or behind in the appropriate training, that logically or empirically invalidates the proposition that professionals are versed in specialized theory and technique (and, we may now add, widely experienced in applying them). Even if the majority of practising professionals are behind in their knowledge of the latest scientific advances, they are not necessarily lacking expert knowledge, nor is their level of expertise necessarily at the same level as that of the laity.

3 *Professionals have a strong sense of identity with their colleagues and a resulting sense of community.* Attribute number 2, as well as attributes 4 through 8, contribute to this sense of identity. Put another way, professionals have a wide range of shared experiences not found to the same degree in other occupations. In addition, there is a strong tendency by each professional group to promote the group's distinctiveness and excellence, both among themselves and outsiders, a process they justify in terms of attributes 1 and 2.

Studies of team-based professionals, such as those in symphony orchestras, dance companies, and football teams, suggest the existence of an even stronger sense of identity and community than is found among independent professionals. As members of a team, they share directly in its successes and failures, whether those stem from the various operating situations or from their experience working as a group through coordinated and cooperative action. In short, collegiality appears to be even better developed here than among the more diffuse "community" of independent, mostly client-centred professionals.

This sense of identity is as evident in the areas of art, science, and sport as in the mainline professions. It is less, although still reasonably, well developed in the entertainment field. The vague boundaries of the various domains of popular entertainment are at the root of this deficiency. A singer might, for example, perform a little magic and stand-up comedy between songs. At times, stand-up comics might work as sketch players or script writers as well. Nonetheless, those who make their living on the entertainment stage share many common experiences, such as unsympathetic or unscrupulous agents and night-club managers, hostile or indifferent audiences, inadequate performing conditions, unconventional (chiefly nocturnal) work hours, high public visibility, similar after-hours leisure practices, and an itinerant lifestyle. First and foremost, entertainers share the difficult goal of amusing audiences in ways that are sufficiently appealing to lead to a career in their art, whether amateur or professional.

4 *Professionals master a generalized cultural tradition associated with their line of work.* This cultural tradition may be stronger in the art, sport, entertainment, and perhaps even the scientific domains than in, say, the legal, medical, or religious areas. One explanation is that, if for no other reason, the publics of the first set have an interest in the respective traditions and, therefore, help to keep them alive. They care about the great names and events in the history of particular sports, arts, and entertainment fields, as attested to by the numerous popular books on these subjects. In contrast, clients are seldom interested in the equivalent in law, medicine, teaching, or architecture.[4] What these latter clients want are solutions to pressing problems in the present. The publics, on the other hand, want some sort of positive stimulation of an artistic, intellectual, or pleasurable sort, a stimulation enhanced by the acquisition of knowledge concerning the cultural tradition of the profession in question.

5 *Professionals use institutionalized means of formally or consensually validating the adequacy of training and trained individuals.* In the client-centred professions, this attribute refers to licences and examinations, which authenticate professional status. The education of professional

scientists, for example, incorporates a similar means for this same purpose; that is, an advanced degree from a recognized educational institution. A more divergent means is found in sports and some arts and entertainment fields, where formal recognition as a professional is established through membership in a professional group or listing, whether that be a symphony orchestra, sports team, or dance company; an agent's "stable" of entertainment artists; or a "list" of professional players (as in tennis and boxing). Artists and entertainers are also validated as professionals when they are invited, or hired, to present their art in places renowned for displaying professional talent. These include celebrated museums, theatres, concert halls, nightclubs, and recording studios. According to this criteria, many of today's young fine artists, even with their university or conservatory degrees, cannot yet be termed professionals. They must first be judged sufficiently qualified to be listed, hired, presented, or represented in the ways just mentioned. It is in this sense that George Bernard Shaw could claim that all professions are a conspiracy against the laity.

Nonetheless, these elaborations of what constitutes the institutionalized validation of professionalism are all formal. There are still many professionals in art and entertainment who have never been validated in this way and who, for example, receive only local recognition from their colleagues that they are of professional quality – a form of consensual (as opposed to institutionalized) validation commonly found in jazz and entertainment magic. Thus, because the formal process is evident only in certain professions, I have modified attribute 5 to read "formally or consensually validating ..."

This is a good point in the discussion to embark on a brief aside as to how, given their frequent lack of formal validation, public-centred professionals in art and entertainment can be operationally defined. It is well known that only a small minority of artists and entertainers can live solely by the income from their vocation (e.g., Standing Committee on Communications and Culture 1989, 9). In 1980, the Federation of American and Canadian Musicians reported that only 10 percent of its members were working full time (*Music Calgary* 1988, 2). A similar figure is available for members of the Actors' Equity Association (Cohen 1990, 11). Most professionals in these fields are forced to be part-time practitioners to some degree. How, then, does one differentiate part-time professionals from amateurs?

To qualify as a professional in my study of magicians, for example, a magician had to meet two of the ideal-typical attributes presented in this chapter. That magician had to be known by local amateurs and professionals for, first, his or her *excellence* as a performer (no. 2) and, second, for his or her *dedication* to magic as an entertainment art (no. 6).[5]

Of the twenty-six who met these criteria, fourteen were considered "part-time professionals," because they held full-time jobs outside the field of magic. For some of the part-timers, their external work was as attractive and important to them as performing magic; for others, that work was a stopgap to be abandoned when full-time employment in their art was achieved. In other words, part-time professionals in magic, in contrast to amateurs, regard their work as at least a second job, if not their principal one. Incidentally, eight of these part-timers had once worked as full-time performers. As John Taylor (1964–6, 18) puts it, all professional artists, both full-time and part-time, whether they intend to make a career of their art or not, are individuals to be imitated, possibly because they set standards and, certainly, because they meet those set by others.

Generally speaking, however, that is a local system of evaluation, one based on the standards of excellence that have diffused from the world centres of the art. It is at the centres where the trail-blazers collect, some of whom may be amateurs (Yates 1964–6). In present-day magic, these centres may be found in London, England, and the Hollywood–Los Angeles area. What constituted excellence and dedication among local magicians was left to the judgment of established professionals known to be familiar with magic in their communities. For this study, I asked at least two of the central figures in each city studied to list their professional colleagues, both part-time and full-time.

6 *Professional work constitutes a calling in which consistent application of a standard and provision of a service, or product, are primary and monetary rewards are secondary.* Given the occurrences today of strikes, slow-downs, and unionization among such professionals as teachers, doctors, and professors, one might wonder if this notion of a calling, in particular, is still a valid indicator of professionalism. In other words, has greed not replaced the selfless commitment of yesteryear?

No definitive research exists with regard to this question. There are certainly signs, however, that the work of such professionals is at least as important to them as the money they gain from it. Although members of the clergy and social workers provide two good examples, fine artists are probably the epitome of the poorly remunerated, committed professional (in dance, photography, and painting, see Goodman 1974, 21; Perreault 1988; Schwartz 1986, 184–5). I also found that the entertainment and sport professionals in the Project generally earned very modest livings (see also Theberge 1980; Kutner 1983; Friedman 1990), having chosen their work because of their profound love for it. Indeed that profound love, or passion, for the pursuits on which the public-centred professions are built (see chapter 6) turns out to be a key attitude, one that distinguishes these professionals from their client-centred counterparts whose love for their work appears to be more moderate. Indeed, how many physicians, lawyers, or schoolteachers would work for the low pay of the typical artist, magician, or basketball player, or, incidentally, for the pure joy of the amateur?

Roth (1974, 10) criticizes the standards, not to mention the service, component of this attribute, by pointing out that client-centred professionals often give inferior service to minority and deviant groups. His criticism does not apply, however, to public-centred professionals. For example, scientists, artists, entertainers, and athletes who fail to meet set standards will suffer public disfavour and a subsequent lack of patronage. Indeed, this can happen even when they do their best. The publics of these professionals are too diffuse to discriminate against in the way described by Roth.

This attribute thus varies between, and possibly within, the two categories of professionals. The empirical question, then, is whether the internal variation among professionals of all kinds is still low enough and therefore closer to the ideal-type than the variations found in other occupational groups. In the meantime, using a code of ethics as an expression of professionalism is of questionable value. It clearly fails to engender a uniformly high quality of service in the client-centred professions, and the question of ethics is simply nonexistent in the public-centred ones. Moreover, as Roth (1974, 10) has noted, such codes are found in "non-professional" work as well. For these reasons, I did not refer to them in the sixth attribute.

Finally, any study of arts, sports, and entertainment professionals underlines the importance of a *consistent* application of standards and service. Apart from the issue of client discrimination in some professions, is the issue, noted especially when comparing amateurs and professionals, of consistently good work. For instance, because public-centred professionals are always presenting their works before more or less the same critical set of consumers, inconsistencies are easily spotted. But inconsistencies are also unexpected. In this regard, professionals are perceived as being "cool" in tough situations; they are thought of as prepared, persevering, experienced and, therefore, unlikely to deliver other than professional quality work *all the time*. In fact, the same is expected of client-centred professionals, even though the clients are seldom organized such that they can monitor this quality. Nonetheless, this latter group of professionals generally appear to expect consistent excellence of themselves and their colleagues.

7 *Professionals are recognized by their clients or publics for their special authority based on their knowledge, technique, and experience.* Roth (1974, 8) holds that this attribute is invalid, in part, because clients sometimes

reject professional advice. However, this is to miss the point: that those who reject professional advice thought highly enough of it to seek it out in the first place. Second, rejection of such advice does not necessarily mean the advice itself is bad; it only means that, for whatever reason, the client dislikes it. Some people reject medical advice, not because they think the physician is incompetent or that they themselves know more, but because they cannot bring themselves to do what the physician advises. To be sure, certain people do think they know more than the professionals (and that may actually be the case). They may even not seek advice, believing that they are acting entirely on rational grounds. An ideal-type analysis would show the prevalence of such rejections across the professions.

Indeed, the wholesale rejection of professional advice seems highly unlikely, given the spheres of life within which professionals operate. Jamous and Peloille (1970) offer two principles by way of explaining this tendency. The first – the principle of indeterminacy, which was mentioned earlier – is that professional knowledge and technique are largely unavailable to the laity. This condition combines with that of acute uncertainty as to how to remedy a pressing problem – or the principle of uncertainty. This situation induces many people to seek the knowledge and techniques of client-centred professionals and, as we shall note later, gives the latter considerable power over the former.

The issue of rejection of authority is unheard of in the public-centred professions, in part because the principle of uncertainty is not found there. Admittedly there are people who dislike basketball, abstract art, stand-up comedy, or entomology. But this rejection is usually a matter of personal preference or taste, rather than of belief in the incompetence of the players, artists, comedians, or scientists. For example, for every professional golfer who fails to win in the main tournaments, there is a local duffer who would be thrilled to spend an afternoon with such a person receiving tips on how to improve his or her game. The attribute of special authority, when approached from an ideal-typical vantage point, shows at least the possibility of being an important component in the definition of professional.

8 *Professional services and products provide an avenue for the attainment of certain important social values.* There appears to be little disagreement as to the significance of this proposition in any definition of professional. Health, well-being, education, artistry, salvation, entertainment, and displays of excellence are among the values that the professionals can offer their clients or publics. Still, an ideal-type analysis would show more precisely how both types of professionals uniquely serve the laity, when compared both with each other and with other classes of occupations.

9 *Professional work is self-regulated*. This component also begs an ideal-type analysis, inasmuch as there are many organizationally based professionals whose autonomy is limited to some significant degree by their employers' demands. Waters's (1989) examination of professional collegiality and bureaucracy makes this point clear. In fact, there is even evidence that some organizations demand that professionals compromise their standards (e.g., Daniels 1969; Waters 1989). One might, indeed, question the amount and kind of autonomy that is available to members of such art, sports, and entertainment groups as orchestras, baseball teams, and comedy troupes. Nevertheless, I did observe some room in these fields for individual judgment (in sport, see Bensman and Lilienfeld 1990, 53–4), including how to coordinate one's own actions with those of other members of the group so as to form a unified and unique product of professional quality (on the lack of individual autonomy in ballet, see Perreault 1988; in music, see Couch 1989, 275). Still, autonomy in these professions seems to be available chiefly at the collective level, as the distinct result of concerted actions of individual specialists.

Stand-up comedy is possibly the purest instance of attribute number 9, given the freedom of its practitioners to write, interpret, and improvise. In reality, the only effective constraints on artistic freedom here are those of the marketplace. For comics, such a constraint refers to whether the audience perceives an act as funny. No matter what the content of the act, if there is laughter, the professional product is good. Certainly no other profession has more autonomy than stand-up comedy, which, according to comic Jerry Seinfeld, explains why comics seek this occupation (Hershon 1990, 17).

POWER AND PROFESSIONS

The attribution approach to the study of professions, particularly its functionalist interpretation, has drawn considerable fire over the past two decades from proponents of an alternative perspective, summarized here under the general heading of the power approach. Roth's (1974) critique, although more extreme than most, is but one example (e.g., Klegon 1978; Hall 1983; Portwood and Fielding 1981). The power theorists have found sufficient weaknesses in the attribution approach to cause several of them to renounce it as useless, if not dangerous. The difficulty appears to be the subtle biases it is held to contain.

One criticism of the attributes is that they are little more than ideological statements of what professions ought to be; that is, statements made by professionals themselves to paint a publicly acceptable picture of their occupations. The attributes-as-ideology approach is said to be used to justify the acquisition and retention of control over such important privileges as training practitioners and delivering service. An extension of this idea is that the acquired power and privilege create a comfortable upper-middle-class position for professionals. According to the power theorists, the functionalists largely ignored such considerations, even though Francis Bacon coined his famous dictum "knowledge is power," nearly 400 years ago.

A second criticism is that the intense interest in the attributes of professions has blinded attribution theorists to the process by which the professions themselves emerge; namely, professionalization (e.g., Caplow 1954; Wilensky 1964; Hughes 1971). The studies of process and power are compatible, say the power theorists, inasmuch as gaining power and control are major developments in the history of certain professions.

A third criticism, closely related to the first two, involves the tendency of the proponents of the attribution approach to ignore the external environment of a profession, both past and present (Klegon 1978). Indeed, say the power theorists, other institutions, organizations, and professions can affect the acquisition and maintenance of power and the development of the attributes themselves.

Many sociologists accept these criticism, thereby pushing power and process to the fore. Ritzer and Walczak (1986, 86) summarize present thought on power and process and the attributes of professions as follows:

Of greatest utility is the constellation of characteristics [attributes] developed by the functionalists. But these can no longer be viewed as necessarily "real" things that professions possess and [other] occupations do not. Rather, they must be seen either a) as traits that are derived from the power of the professions and are of secondary importance, or b) as a set of deceptive "traits" that the professions do not actually possess but have been able to convince significant others that they have. Thus the constellation of characteristics can be real, mythical, or some combination of the two. The structural-functional approach remains useful, but as an adjunct to a power-process model.

PUBLIC-CENTRED PROFESSIONS

The question that remains unanswered is whether the public-centred professions are truly professions. From our review of the nine attributes in terms of the Project studies, the public-centred professionals seem to fulfil all but one attribute – number 5, the formal and consensual validation of training and competence; this lack seems, moreover, to hold more for artists and entertainers than for scientists and athletes.

As for the principles of indeterminacy and uncertainty, only the former applies to the public-centred professions. The very presence of amateurs attests to the weak control these professionals have over their domain. Clearly, they fail to monopolize their own training and productions, and, as we shall see in chapter 4, their publics often exert a measure of control over the production aspect. Indeed, as Judith Adler (1975, 369) describes the situation in the fine arts: "Market success, though unpredictable and determined by laymen, becomes the final arbiter of colleagueship, the final validation of a product as art and of its maker as an artist."

Saks (1983) holds that sociologists by and large agree on the definition of professions as legally privileged groups that have gained considerable monopolistic control over the social and economic opportunities affecting their fate. Abbott (1988, 7) concludes from his review that there is widespread agreement that a profession is a more or less exclusive, specialized occupational group formed around an abstract skill that requires extensive training. The skill, he says, is applied on a case-by-case basis.[6] Together, these two definitions include many more of the attributes than at least some contemporary theorists would appear to accept. Nonetheless, the question remains as to the status of the public-centred professions: are they simply another set of occupations, or are they a special form of professional work in their own right? Indeed, the two definitions fail to offer much help here, inasmuch as they rest on a small amount of research and a large amount of arm-chair theorizing (much of which is highly ideological and anti-professions [Saks 1983, 9–11]). Clearly, researchers will have to settle whether the attributes are real or ideological. It is rare, moreover, for either the theory or research – what there is of it – to address the professional status of those who work in art, science, sport, and entertainment.

Given the dearth of research and the presence of theoretical bias, it is unwise to foreclose just yet on the public-centred professions, saying, categorically, that they are not really professions. Indeed, I know of no research in sociology comparing professions and non-professions along the lines of the nine attributes. Yet from the studies that made up this Project, I am convinced that the professional attributes in the areas of art, science, sport, and entertainment are real, not ideological. But I have not made comparisons with other types of occupations, for example, those in management or the trades. If such comparisons were to reveal that public-centred professions fall significantly closer to the ideal-typical attributes than other occupations, I would have to seriously question the central role claimed for power and control by contemporary sociologists. As we have seen, that group argues that power and control are the essence of all professions – a stance difficult to defend if public-centred professions turn out to be substantially different from other occupations, but still similar to the client-centred professions in all aspects except that of power.[7]

By the way, from the evidence at hand, the public-centred professions would seem to fit the definition of a marginal profession quite poorly; that is, of an occupation striving to be recognized as professional that is nevertheless denied this status by more powerful professions whose vested interests are threatened by such aspirations. My studies suggest that, in general, public-centred professionals have little interest in such recognition; rather they assume they have it and give the matter little further thought. They are most concerned with the quality of their work, its reception by the public, and the pursuit, often against heavy odds, of a professional career. In other words, it is much more important to be seen as an excellent and committed artist, athlete, scientist, or entertainer than as a member of an exclusive group that controls the conditions of excellence and commitment. Moreover, there appears to be scant interest in the possibility of jurisdictional control of the public-centred professions by other occupational groups, unless one includes in this process the efforts of labour unions to set their own boundaries. For the most part, however, unions play a small role in organizing and controlling occupational activities in these four areas.

For the present, then, it is better to divide the study of professions into two categories. The first is the *client-centred professions*, where monopolistic control over training and service is one attribute (possibly a quintessential one at that) of a set of occupations that form in problematic areas of life where uncertainty is too acute to permit unfettered, free enterprise service to supply the remedy. We need control in these areas, which we have granted, in substantial degree, to the professions. Here one could treat power, as Ritzer and Walczak (1986, 78) have suggested, as another, let us say the *tenth*, attribute of professions, albeit the one from which the other nine may turn out to be derived. But, since all this can apply only to client-centred professions, a second category is necessary; namely, the *public-centred* professions. These latter form in expressive areas of life, where there is no acute uncertainty and where, as a result, no one has been given the right of control, especially the professions themselves.

These two categories can, unfortunately, guide research on the professions only in democratic societies that are largely or wholly capitalistic. Yet within this restriction, the twofold classification has the advantage of enabling power and control to be placed within a broader context, thereby showing how this attribute is itself controlled, held to certain spheres of life where its presence is believed to be justified.

Begun (1986, 122–3) describes how this process works in economic terms in his discussion of the professions in the market place. Abbott's (1988) "ecological" perspective highlights the importance of culture, public opinion, and legal and administrative rules as limitations on professional activity. The concept of deprofessionalization has recently been developed to describe the impact of these contextual, or environmental, forces (Ritzer and Walczak 1986, 89–93). The extent of this control on the use of power should also be explored, by comparing the professional attributes, with their equivalents in other occupations, at all levels of prestige and socioeconomic status.

CONCLUSIONS

We leave this chapter as we entered it, with a discussion of definitions. There is no doubt that, to the extent that the attribution approach has served as a guide to research – and not just a definition – it has had its limitations. But, to refer once more to Freidson, we must have some sort of definition of professional with which to focus our research. Unfortunately, the "folk" definition he proposes – that a group is professional when it claims to be and when it somehow justifies this claim (Freidson 1983a, 28–36) – will simply not do. How can we speak about the presence or absence of professionalism without some sort of criteria for determining what a professional is and is not? Furthermore, as we shall see later, amateurs frequently claim to be professional; that is, they frequently argue that they are, in certain ways, like the professionals in their fields.

Without some kind of definition of professional, no matter how empirically inadequate it may turn out to be upon further research, the study of amateurs is cut adrift in a sea of conceptual ambiguity. Without a definition of professional, there are no landmarks with which to orient the study of amateurism. That situation is only exacerbated by the fact that amateurs are marginal to the spheres of work and leisure. Yet amateurs do occupy a unique place in modern society.

CHAPTER THREE

Amateurs

Our macrosociological definition of the amateur and the conception of the PAP system point to a far more complicated set of relations between amateurs and professionals than common sense would have us believe. Conventional wisdom holds that amateurs are but one kind of leisure participant who, although perhaps a bit quaint because of their intensity, seem to function, like other leisure participants, independently of any work role. In reality, the relationship between the worlds of leisure and work for amateurs is quite different.

PROFESSIONAL-AMATEUR-PUBLIC RELATIONSHIPS

Amateurs are related to professionals or publics, or both, in at least seven ways. First, amateurs can also be described ideal-typically, in terms of the first nine attributes used in chapter 2 to describe professionals. True, only a few amateurs ever achieve the highest expression of attributes 2 (specialized knowledge), 4 (cultural traditions), 6 (calling), and 7 (special authority) but, as I note later, this is really a question of parallel graduation. In other words, both groups are clearly more advanced in their fields than are their publics; moreover, the good amateurs are better than mediocre professionals.

In effect, then, amateurs serve publics as do professionals and, at times, even the same ones. Amateurs are also oriented by standards of excellence set and communicated by the latter. By way of example, consider the university baseball team that plays before a set of spectators, some of whom turn up the following week at a professional game. But there are also situations, as in theatre, for instance, in which the local public has little opportunity to take in anything other than an amateur production.

Second, a monetary and organizational relationship is frequently established when professionals educate, train, direct, coach, advise, organize, and even perform with amateurs, and when amateurs come to comprise part of their public (in music see Finnegan 1989, 18; in the arts in general, see Smith 1979). For example, among the spectators watching a professional baseball game one week after the amateurs' game, will be found some of those same amateurs. Likewise, when a professional theatre company visits the community where an amateur theatre group usually performs, many of the latter will certainly attend that performance. Similarly, amateurs play with professionals in "pro-am" bowling and in squash, tennis, and golf open tournaments. Indeed, these two types are often members of the same community orchestra or theatrical group. As for the scientific domain, amateurs' projects are reported in professional journals as well as in journals devoted exclusively or partly to their own work (e.g., *The Local Historian, Sky and Telescope, The Bulletin of the Amateur Entomologists' Society*).

Third, there is an intellectual relationship among amateurs, professionals, and publics, that springs primarily from the amateur population. Having more time for such things, amateurs can maintain a broader knowledge of their activity than can most professionals. Professionals are often too busy polishing their technique, in effect making a living with that technique, to find time to read about the history of their endeavour or about the forms, styles, periods, or persons beyond their immediate bailiwick (Downes 1951; Barzun 1954, 22, 24–5; Drinker 1967). Although there is a tendency even among amateurs toward specialization and limitation (Barzun 1956a, 438), those who avoid such restrictions can give professionals and publics alike a perspective on the activity. They can also promote a common language for discussion and criticism and work against the breakup of the profession into exclusive subdivisions. Thus, whereas professionals must specialize to succeed, amateurs need not.

Magic offers one example of that intellectual relationship which, here, takes two principal expressions. The first is reflected in reading, an activity amateurs have more time for than professionals. The younger amateurs, for example, are especially prodigious readers, particularly in the history of magic, the biographies of its prominent figures (Houdini is a favourite), and the technical side of the art (e.g., show-business lore, performance tips, new tricks and apparatus). The second is reflected in performing. As performers, both amateurs and professionals tend to specialize chiefly in stage magic or close-up (see also Nardi 1983, 8; Prus and Sharper 1991, 230). The amateurs, however, are considerably more likely than the professionals to devote additional leisure time to experimenting and possibly dabbling with other magic specialities.

Amateurs, as special members of the public, know better than the run-of-the-mill member what constitutes a creditable performance or product. After all, they are trying to meet high standards in their own fashion. They consequently relate to both the public and the professionals in three additional ways: they criticize the professionals for overemphasizing technique and stressing superficialities in lieu of meaningful or profound work; they insist everywhere on the retention of excellence; and they furnish professionals with the stimulus to give the public the best they can (in music see Drinker 1952, 577).

For instance, although a home run in baseball or a $20,000-dollar Stradivarius violin may impress many of the assembled public, amateurs can tell when such trappings are superficial. Clearly, hitting home runs is not always the best strategy for winning a game; nor does an old and famous instrument a musician make. Amateurs can insist on good taste in, say, professional basketball, by demanding a rule that requires players to shoot within a specified time period, instead of stalling; just as they can insist that they be given genuine art rather than some put-on. Or take musicians: they know that a member of the audience who follows a miniature score of a symphony is quite likely to spot any mistakes, spiritless solos, late entries, and other artistic flaws.[1] Often, a sprinkling of skilled, knowledgable, and concerned people among the spectators, readers, audience, or other publics is sufficient to draw the best from performing professionals.

Nevertheless, the evidence from the four studies that considered both professionals and amateurs is that amateur views of this sort fall on deaf ears. That is, in art and entertainment, where amateur-professional interaction is closest, there is an obvious tendency for the professionals to ignore the amateurs' criticism. In my study, while some professional magicians and stand-up comics said they sought and accepted constructive criticism wherever they could find it, including from amateurs, most were inclined to brush off criticism not from professionals as uninformed. This may, however, be a general orientation for these professionals, for they also said that critiques from professional colleagues were often wide of the mark. Also, in sport and science, professionals can avoid association with amateurs. Indeed, many have little or no contact with amateurs once they enter professional circles. Hence, amateurs' views of their activities rarely reach them.

The seventh systematic relationship, this time solely among professionals and amateurs, concerns career paths. Professionals who are part of a PAP system typically start out as amateurs and, unless they abandon their pursuit entirely or die in this role, they return to that status, possibly in the final stage of their career. So far, as the astronomy study demonstrated, science is the only exception to this rule. In that discipline, at least, only a small proportion of professionals come up through the amateur ranks. Indeed, 20 percent of the sample traced their decision to seek a career in astronomy to the appeal of observation, the principal interest of amateurs. The remaining 80 percent became interested in astronomy as the result of the courses and reading undertaken while at university, or later as professional physicists. This subject is treated in greater detail in a subsequent section.

IMPLICATIONS

The foregoing discussion of the PAP system has a number of implications that can help sharpen our conception of the amateur still further. In reality, it is a term that remains imprecise in everyday parlance, being applied to people with little in common, such as critics, practitioners, consumers (audiences, spectators, and the like), and self-styled experts.

One implication is that amateurs engage part-time in activities that, for other people, constitute full-time work roles. One cannot be an amateur butterfly catcher or matchbook collector, for instance; no opportunity for full-time employment exists in those areas. Such forms of leisure, as noted in chapter 1, are actually hobbies, which lie outside any PAP system.

It follows that amateurs are normally adults, although in some fields they may be older teenagers as well (as happened in the study of magicians). In general, however, only other adults can be functionally related to professionals in the ways set forth earlier. Thus, children's activities are best described not by the term "amateur," but by other descriptors, such as "youth" orchestra, "peewee" hockey, "children's" art, and so forth.

A third implication is that, even for amateurs, there is nearly always a public. Perhaps they (as well as professionals) imagine a public some minor proportion of the time. And their real public may be small, composed of friends, relatives, neighbours, or other amateurs engaged in the same activity. Nonetheless, much of the time most amateurs are serving a public, not simply themselves. In fact, many pursuits are unavoidably social, inasmuch as they can only be carried out collectively. Lone piano players, however, are excluded from this aspect of amateur life. In this one significant way, they are not amateurs at all.

Both the PAP system and common sense usage imply that the term "amateur" should be used only with those activities that constitute, for somebody, a *professional* work role. That is, there must be a professional counterpart to the status of amateur. As the preceding chapter shows, judgments of an occupation as either professional or non-professional can, unfortunately, be quite tenuous; new professions are constantly emerging and no profession, even an established one, perfectly fits the ten attributes. Nevertheless, within these limitations, we can say, for example, that, currently, one is simply a canoeist, for there seems to be no professional counterpart to set the high standards that are attainable only through full-time involvement. As stated previously, it is the pursuit of these standards, with some measure of success, that distinguishes the modern amateurs from their predecessors, the gentlemen, and – it may be added here – from all other participants in leisure activities. Amateur tennis players, for example, only appeared after World War II, and simply because the number of professionals began to grow at that time (Kutner 1983). We might also speak of amateur cabinetmakers or gardeners, but only if those people who earn their living in this manner could be said, according to sociological principles, to be professionals. If full-time participants in these activities fail to meet the sociological standards of a profession, or if there are no full-time participants, the part-time enthusiasts are more accurately described as hobbyists than as modern amateurs. With this qualification in mind, it should be possible to eliminate some of the confusion engendered by Bliss Perry (1904, 10–20) who, incidentally, is the first to have written a book on amateurs in general.

The fifth implication revolves around the attribute of professionals and, to a lesser degree, amateurs possessing a widespread knowledge of a specialized technique. To qualify as experts or practitioners, both groups must use that knowledge and technique often enough to avoid their degeneration. Put differently, even the idea of amateur presupposes some level of consistently active usage of the core skills and knowledge of a field. Today's extensive leisure makes this possible.[2]

Teachers in a profession (e.g., dance teachers, swimming instructors), to the extent that they maintain their technique and knowledge in order to teach well, can be considered practitioners. But such people as critics, conductors, producers, directors, non-playing coaches, and full-time administrators who let technique and knowledge atrophy, may not only lose their claim to professional status, but also find themselves without amateur status. As they shift their involvement to another occupation, they move to the periphery of their PAP system; they may also remain in the PAP system, albeit chiefly as members of its public.

Inside this system, but outside amateur circles, are the *dabblers*: those whose active involvement, technique, and knowledge are so meagre as barely to distinguish them from the public of which they are actually a part.[3] Undoubtedly every PAP system has a certain percentage of dabblers, even the scientific area, with its books containing instructions on how to amuse oneself with simple scientific procedures (e.g., Moore and Viorst 1961; Swezey 1948). Roland Barthes (1975, 70) describes dabbling on the piano:

At the piano, "fingering" has nothing to do with an assigned value of elegance and delicacy (which we refer to as "touch") but merely designates a way of numbering the fingers which must play this or that note; fingering establishes in a deliberate manner what will become an automatism: in short, it is the programming of a machine, an animal inscription. Now, if I play badly – aside from the lack of velocity, which is a purely muscular problem – it is because I fail to abide by the written fingering: I improvise, each time I play, the position of my fingers, and therefore I can never play anything without making mistakes. The reason for this is obviously that I want an immediate pleasure and reject the tedium of training, for training hampers pleasure – for the sake of a greater ulterior pleasure, as they say (we tell the pianist what the gods said to Orpheus: Don't turn back *prematurely* on the effects of your action). So that the piece, in the perfection attributed to it but never really attained, functions as a bit of hallucination: I gladly give myself up to the watchword of fantasy: "*Immediately!* " even at the cost of a considerable loss of reality.

Every PAP system also has *novices* among its public, people who may someday be amateurs, possibly even professionals. They are beginners who consistently pursue the activity (thus they are not mere dabblers), but who have yet to grow sufficiently proficient and knowledgable to lay claim to the identity of amateur or professional. Indeed, neither dabblers nor novices are apt to refer to themselves as practitioners in their activity, which is one way of distinguishing them from amateurs. Statements such as "I'm just learning to sculpt" or "I just fool around at golf" identify these participants. In other words, amateurs, while recognizing their limitations, identify themselves as more seriously involved.[4] As one amateur musician put it: "It is time to recognize that amateurs are not necessarily novices. Everybody has to start as a novice, including even composers, and conductors; they do not need to remain so. If they are willing to study, practise, and to learn, they will build in something for good ... Toscanini was one of the Great Amateurs: he loved the music with the divine passion of the saint. I don't claim anything at these altitudes, being a very gentle and I hope, non-fanatical, amateur. But I can testify to the determination to play it well (Marsh 1972, 168–9)."

A sixth implication derives from the etymological roots of the word "amateur;" as an *amator*, he or she is one who loves. This definition, often naïvely used, needs qualification. First, although it is possible, as sometimes claimed, that amateurs are attracted to their pursuits more than their professional colleagues are (perhaps because they engage in them less often), the activity is nevertheless rarely an unalloyed joy for either category. Amateurs do get tired, bored, frustrated, peeved, and discouraged just as professionals do; the acquisition, maintenance, and expression of skill and knowledge always entails some of these feelings. Take the world of the avocational archaeologist, for instance. Excavation is arduous. Digging, hauling, and sifting dirt for hours on end in an environment of heat, insects, sandburs, and humidity require stamina and devotion to archaeology that inevitably deters some novices. More than once I have heard comments about how the speaker would rebel against such labour were it required of him as work or obligatory non-work.

Second, it is common to infer from this definition that professionals dislike their work, apparently because they *have* to do it to live. But this stance fails to square with the sixth ideal-typical attribute of professionals (especially the public-centred ones); namely, that they place standards and service ahead of material rewards. In addition, both professionals and amateurs often find the competition in their fields exhilarating, if not attractive (Perry 1904, 10; for a negative view, see Allison and Meyer 1988). In actuality, professional work, or at least public-centred professional work, is so engaging that it becomes an end in itself, erasing the lines between work and leisure (Pavalko 1988, 187; Parker 1974, 78). Or as T.H. Marshall phrased it: "The professional ... does not work in order to be paid; he is paid in order that he may work" (in Gross 1958, 79). Generally speaking, then, although amateurs love their pursuits or they would not pursue them, it is erroneous to assume that professionals dislike theirs. Indeed, many modern amateurs and professionals are highly dedicated to their particular line of activity, and that is part of its appeal. As a case in point, the strike in 1990 by professional baseball players fizzled partly because many players simply yearned to play baseball (*Calgary Herald* 1990, F3). Or consider the outlook of the professional ballet dancer (Perreault 1988, 182): "Therefore, how can one accept conditions of life and work that are so difficult (excessively long and intensive training, quasi-monastic discipline, pain and suffering nearly every day because of numerous injuries, etc.), remuneration that often borders on poverty, total absence of employment security and a retirement plan, when, to be sure, that retirement comes so early? After having interviewed eighty male and female dancers, we do not hesitate to answer: through *passion*. These artists are passionate beings ready to sacrifice all to experience their passion" (author's translation). The sentiment of the ballet dancer is shared by many other types of artists, both fine and popular (Lacroix 1990, 12).

Love for and dedication to an activity are inevitably somewhat different for and among amateurs and professionals. For example, sportspeople – Charnofsky (1968) has shown this for major league baseball players, and Theberge (1980) for female golfers – enjoy many aspects of their professional lives, such as the money and travel, the meeting of people, even the attractiveness of the game itself. In contrast, because no amateurs, whatever their interest, are involved in their activities as a way of life, it is the central activity itself that must attract. Both groups can honestly say that they enjoy their pursuits, but for sets of reasons that only partially overlap.

The seventh implication is that amateur involvement in an activity is possible only when the training, licencing, and equipment are available to those who intend to make it an avocation. Few people are likely to go through the rigours of formal medical training, for instance, just to practise medicine as an amateur, whereas those without this training would be refused legal recognition for such practice. The practice of amateur law, medicine, education, nursing, and the like are, for the most part, legal impossibilities, according to my definition of amateurism. Added to this is the fact that one never hears these professional activities referred to as amateur in everyday conversation, unless by "amateur" the speaker means "quack" or "imposter." Indeed, the training for policemen and airline pilots, in that it is less rigorous than training for physicians, is more available to would-be amateurs. But official authorization to assume such roles would be denied amateurs, as would the necessary equipment, such as uniforms, badges, patrol cars, and commercial airplanes. Thus, there can be neither amateur policemen nor amateur airline pilots unless, as the police have done in isolated instances, citizen patrol units are given official authorization (e.g., US National Institute of Law Enforcement and Criminal Justice 1977; *Calgary Herald* 1988).

This implication concerns the power of many client-centred professions and the validity of attribute number 10. Such groups have the capacity to prevent the amateur practice of their activities, which is why client-centred professionals who practise part-time are best labelled part-time professionals rather than pure or post-professional amateurs (see next section). Certainly, certification, and all that that involves, precludes amateur participation, whatever the amount of time devoted to the activity. Part-time, client-centred professionals might include the psychiatrist who moves into hospital administration but still sees a few patients from time to time, or the nurse who works a couple of night shifts each week to supplement family income. To the extent that we can validly classify full-time military personnel as professionals, their part-time counterparts in reserves and militias could also be termed, by the same logic, part-time professionals (see Zurcher and Harries-Jenkins 1978).

TYPES OF MODERN AMATEURS

A theoretical undertaking, such as the present one, can make little real progress without a typology. Although no doubt there are other dimensions to the question of choosing such a tool, the library sources supporting the original version of the theory (Stebbins 1977), the eight field studies, and everyday speech all point to two important dimensions along which distinctions can be drawn. Perhaps the most important of these is the dimension of seriousness. When amateurs are highly dedicated to their pursuits we may refer to them as *devotees*. When they are only moderately interested, but significantly more so than dabblers, we may call them *participants*. Participants greatly outnumbered devotees in seven of the eight studies, stand-up comedy being the exception. This dimension can be distinguished operationally by the amount of time the participants commit to practising, rehearsing, performing, and studying, in accordance with the accepted professional norms for the pursuit.[5]

The second dimension concerns career paths. The *pre-professionals* are amateurs who intend to join the professional ranks. The *pure amateurs* have never seriously held such aspirations; or, if they have, they have failed for some reason to enter those ranks. The *post-professionals*, although they have decided to abandon their profession, still wish to participate in its activities on a part-time basis. Post-professionals reach this status by retiring, accepting employment peripheral to their PAP system, or switching to a career in a different field (e.g., the discouraged professional jazz musician who turns to insurance sales, but continues to attend jam sessions). No doubt there are other paths as well.

A special career category of *conditional pre-professional* emerged in the Texas baseball study as well as in the later Canadian studies of magicians and stand-up comics. In response to questions about future plans, some amateurs had said that they were considering becoming professionals in their field, if certain conditions were met. In fact, this category probably exists in all four amateur-professional areas under consideration here. The following conditional statements were typical: "I will turn professional 'if I get an offer from a professional scout (baseball)'; 'if I make enough money to subsist' (magic, stand-up comedy); 'if I earn a doctoral degree' (science); or 'if I pass the audition for a particular role'" (art). I shall have more to say in chapter 5 about this conditional orientation toward the amateur-professional career.

Six types of amateurs resulted from cross-classifying these two dimensions. Both the pre-professional devotees and the participants drew attention to the fact that amateurs gradually form a major pool from which professionals are recruited (with the exceptions mentioned earlier). Schools of music, art, and dance explicitly train for this purpose, although, interestingly, a number of writers felt that the music schools should also train pure amateur devotees (e.g., Hendrickson 1968; Boutilier 1969). In fact, at least one music school does just that (Bain 1967, 114). Community orchestras and, to some extent, summer stock and amateur theatres (Manning and Hearn 1969, 203) help develop future professionals as well. Also undergraduate programs in the sciences produce numerous amateurs. Some of these science graduates continue their education, becoming professionals; others use it in such a way as to contribute nothing new to the field; a smaller third group (of devotees) manages to make new contributions despite this modest formal background. In addition, recruitment of professional athletes from university teams is a well-known practice.[6] In the individual sports, among them golf, squash, and tennis, advanced amateurs are suddenly transformed into professionals through certification by the association that controls their sport. The movement of amateurs to professional status is generally more gradual, however, in a game such as chess or in the entertainment field. Stand-up comedy, however, is an exception: here amateurs are "promoted" by an agent to the status of opening act and paid the minimal professional wage. In addition, some magicians are suddenly vaulted into professional status after signing contracts of several months' duration; their goal is to perform on a cruise ship or with a circus.

Pre-professional amateurs are valid serious leisure practitioners. Although they are learning to become professionals, they are doing so in a pursuit they have freely chosen, at which they are still unable to make a living, and from which they derive a great deal of enjoyment. Included in this category are the students in university undergraduate and pre-professional programs whose value commitment (see next section) is relatively high and whose continuance commitment has not yet taken root. In short, as in all leisure, pre-professional amateurs can renounce their pursuits. Such a delineation excludes graduate students and students in professional programs, who are more accurately described as junior professionals upgrading their occupational qualifications through further training and experience. They are capable of performing certain professional tasks and may even be paid to do this during their student years. This delineation also excludes, for similar reasons, the state-supported, "elite amateur" athletes (e.g., Olympic athletes), who are really junior and sometimes not-so-junior professionals. There are, of course, undergraduate and pre-professional students who look on their educational careers as an extensive non-work obligation; they are hardly amateurs.

The distinction between devotees and participants, whatever their placement along the career dimension, indicates that amateurs differ within the same field in terms of their dedication and, it follows, in terms of their development and expression of skill and knowledge. This same distinction, of course, could also be drawn vis-à-vis professionals, although, in general, the required levels of skill, knowledge, and dedication would be somewhat higher (in sport see Weiss 1969, 201). According to Barzun (1954, 21), a profession is not a company of mutually respectful equals, but instead is a continuum of imperfect aspirants to perfection. He goes on to explain: "A parallel gradation necessarily obtains among amateurs, and it follows that by applying rigorously any test of pure talent one would find many an amateur high up among the professionals and many a professional down among the duffers."

Although it is moderately possible to find post-professional devotees in the scientific arena, it's almost impossible to do so in the area of strenuous sports. Such people are most apt to appear in the arts, where, as musicians, they play in chamber music groups and community orchestras or, as actors and actresses, they seek parts in amateur productions. Many artists, moreover, including sculptors, painters, writers, and even some musicians, being independent entrepreneurs, never retire (Hearn 1972). The same may be said for entertainers.

All in all, pre-professional *participants* stand the best chance of failing when they reach the professional world and, thus, of being forced to accept prematurely the status of post-professional participant. Indeed, they may even fail to get started professionally. In any case, they are forever participants, as in the case of the male, university baseball player who, snubbed by the professional teams, winds up playing in a municipal league, while making his living at another line of work. He thus becomes a pure amateur participant.

ATTITUDES

Up to this point, we have been discussing the macrosociological definition of amateurs: amateurs as part of a professional-amateur-public system of relations and relationships. A social-psychological definition is also possible, and it is to the development of such a definition that I now turn.

I approach the task by discussing five attitudes, each of which is a variation by which amateurs are separated from professionals and both are separated from their publics (including dabblers and novices). They include: confidence, perseverance, continuance commitment, preparedness, and self-conception. It should be emphasized that the variations that separate amateurs from professionals represent only matters of degree. We have already discussed other attitudes; namely, dedication to and love for the field, as well as identity with one's colleagues; amateurs and professionals are too much alike in these orientations, however, for them to serve as adequate differentiators.

Confidence

Confidence is typically high among experienced professionals, but comparatively low among most amateurs (in sport see Weiss 1969, 201–5). For instance, numerous questions and commentaries dart through the typical amateur's mind: Is this scientific finding significant? Is this the correct entry for my solo? What if I should fall while doing this dance step? I get so nervous in overtime that I lose control of the ball. Amateurs, more than seasoned professionals, doubt their abilities, express them timidly, lose control through nervous tension, and the like. I found that professionals also experience nervousness (see chapter 6) but, as actress Catherine Cornell points out: "You learn to control it better all the time" (in Funke and Booth 1961, 200).

The Project added some important detail to this statement, although chiefly in connection with nervousness, or stage fright. Stage fright is an emotional state that arises apropos the problem of sustaining an identity in the face of apprehensiveness about one's ability to do so. It develops when performers or players know, in advance, that their performance – particularly any slip, flaw, or failure – could bring scrutiny from others (Lyman and Scott 1989; Stebbins 1981a).

In fact, nervousness was not usually a problem in the largely non-performance pursuits, including all avocational science. The only mention of it here was its occurrence prior to the delivery of a scientific paper at a club meeting or scholarly conference. It was a problem for only a minority of avocational scientists and then only before their first two or three presentations.

"Jitters" or "nerves," as they were referred to in football and baseball, were a far more common phenomenon. In general, the higher the level of play, the more likely the player was to report pre-game jitters. The vast majority of baseball and football players on professional, university, and municipal teams were beset by this emotion before each game. About half the Canadian junior football players said they, too, were nervous at this time. In the typical case, nervousness ends and confidence returns once the game gets underway and the player has made his or her first appearance.

The patterns of stage fright vary extensively for drama and entertainment. In theatre and stand-up comedy, approximately half the amateurs and professionals noted considerable nervousness before going onstage. In magic, the proportion in both categories was close to 80 percent. What accounts for these differences in levels of nervousness between magic and football, on the one hand, and theatre and stand-up comedy, on the other? The answer may lie in the nature of the pursuits themselves. The first two require the physical manipulation of people or objects, either of which could prove resistant and lead to failure onstage. Presenting lines – the very essence of drama and stand-up comedy – usually lacks this component of manipulation, although the possibility of forgetting them is enough to engender stage fright in a certain proportion of these practitioners.

In every area, including even avocational science, exceptional circumstances can elevate nervousness. A crucial game, a new magic trick, a distracted audience (say, because of scantily clad waitresses), or a thespian's persistent cough are among the special conditions that can momentarily lower confidence and raise nervousness. What is exceptional or special depends, to be sure, upon the definition of each practitioner's situation. But within their different ranges of experience, amateurs are generally no more inclined than professionals in the same field to define a performance or playing circumstances as frightening. Thus, the Project confirmed that what separates the two in terms of confidence was not the proportion of tense playing and performing situations, but the professionals' superior capacity to control the associated potentially debilitating emotion. This superior control, as well as the professionals' wide experience in the pursuit lead, in turn, to greater confidence.

Perseverance

Different levels of perseverance similarly distinguish amateurs and professionals. Professionals, whether seasoned or green, know they must stick to their pursuit when the going gets tough (in the arts see Collingwood 1958, 313–14). Assisting them here is the professional subculture. Their fellow professionals help them interpret vituperative comments from critics, coaches, conductors, directors, editors, and others – comments that amateurs are less likely to get, if they get them at all. By pointing out how progress will resume in the future if certain steps are taken, members of the professional subculture also encourage professionals to persist at shaping skills that seem to have reached a plateau. In addition, certain tricks of the trade that facilitate progress circulate among the professionals, only infrequently seeping down to the amateurs. One of these, found in certain professional sports, is how to foul an opposing player without detection by the officials, a tactic that helps control the player. Finally, injuries, especially a series of them, can be discouraging for any athlete, professional, or amateur. Again, the former are aided, not only by continuous encouragement from colleagues, but by specialized equipment and personnel that help ensure the fastest recovery possible.

The various studies in this Project revealed that both amateurs and professionals find considerable reason to persevere. Although the prevalence of this attitude was found to be more or less the same for both types, the nature of the perseverance was different. Amateurs can be choosy, professionals cannot. To live, the latter must accept all the available work that comes along, at least until a surplus of opportunities occurs, at which point one can choose the most appealing. This observation is particularly valid for entertainers and fine artists.

In sport, differences in perseverance were evident in management's demands that professionals play despite serious injury or illness. Amateurs, realizing that playing under these conditions is potentially injurious to long-term health, can refuse such demands. Professionals, bolstered by pain-killing drugs, have similar thoughts; yet faced with the need to make a living, not to mention the pressure of coaches and managers that they sacrifice for the good of the team, they more often acquiesce.

Commitment

The greater perseverance of professionals is fostered, in part, by their greater commitment to continuance. The concept of "continuance commitment," developed by Becker (1960), Kantor (1969), and Stebbins (1970b; 1971), is defined as "the awareness of the impossibility of choosing a different social identity ... because of the imminence of penalties involved in making the switch" (Stebbins 1971, 35). Although continuance commitment to a professional identity is a self-enhancing matter – one is forced to remain in a status to which one is attracted – penalties still militate against its renunciation. For example, for some professionals such movement is limited by seniority, legal contracts, and pension funds. Others may have made expensive investments of time, energy, and money in obtaining training and equipment. With few exceptions, amateurs experience these sorts of pressures much less often. Whereas they typically have a strong "value commitment" but a weaker continuance commitment (Stebbins 1970), professionals typically are strongly committed in both ways.

The Project disclosed that, as one might expect, it takes a certain amount of time for amateurs to develop a significant value commitment to their pursuit. At the beginning of their leisure careers, amateurs are inclined to experiment with and evaluate the activity to determine what they can gain from it. They begin to approach the level of value commitment found among professionals in the same field once they find a consistent, favourable ratio of rewards to costs. Beginning amateurs are thus less committed on a value basis than more experienced amateurs or full-fledged professionals.

As indicated, professionals experience a greater continuance commitment than amateurs who, like all leisure participants, are free to "opt out." The Project demonstrated, however, that professionals have more routes available through which to escape discontent than do amateurs. Some professional scientists, for example, have an opportunity to assume administrative roles while continuing their research. Established professional comics can maintain a part-time involvement in live comedy while writing film scripts, performing commercials, or acting in television sketches. The fine artist might teach as well as perform (or write or paint) or, as happens in music, become involved in union affairs. None of these options is open to amateurs. Only in sport do the career options for amateurs and professionals resemble each other.

It should be clear by this point that commitment to a serious leisure pursuit is not necessarily incompatible with freedom to choose the pursuit, for participants have a value, rather than a continuance, commitment to it. Shamir (1988, 250–1) notes that leisure commitment still allows freedom of choice as to the activity itself, as well as freedom of behaviour while pursuing it. I have encountered cases, for example, in which participants have renounced a pursuit at certain points in their leisure careers. Of course, it would be awkward, on several counts, to quit a theatre company just before performances began, but one can always quit at the end of the theatre season.

Preparedness

Professionals also evince a greater preparedness than amateurs. "Preparedness" refers to a readiness to perform the activity to the best of one's ability at the appointed time and place. It also refers to punctuality at such events as rehearsals and games and to participation in these events, not only in appropriate physical condition (not worn out from a day's work, or woozy from too many beers beforehand) but also with the required equipment suitably adjusted and in good repair. Sir John Gielgud stated the case for professional acting: "The discipline of an actor is getting there every day a good hour before you go on, which I usen't to do when I was young, but which I would not dream of not doing now..." (in Funke and Booth 1961, 21). Amateur cellist Leonard Marsh (1972, 127) describes how he was unprepared to play in a chamber music concert:

I ... signified my readiness to play, and we started. It was only then that I found that, in my haste, I hadn't put on my music glasses. My music glasses are carefully adjusted to read cello music at just the right distance ... I could manage fairly well by cocking my head at an awkward angle, but if I did it too much, it would look as if I were querying the interpretation of my companions ... toward the end of the movement I felt confident enough to take my eyes off the music and "look natural." That was the mistake: I lost the vision of a whole line of music, and started playing the wrong notes.

In addition, the studies showed that such obligations as work, family, school, and friendship, separately or in combination, can undermine amateurs' plans to remain well prepared. For example musicians whose jobs demand that they work an extra hour the day the civic orchestra rehearses have little time to practise before tackling the difficult parts that evening. The fact that many amateur activities are scheduled during late weekday afternoons or early evenings presents another problem: fatigue. Although a large majority of amateurs talked about looking forward to their after-hours leisure pursuits, they also talked about fatigue as an obstacle to doing one's best.

Preparedness is also affected by the monetary side of serious leisure. Fees, repairs, lessons, equipment, babysitters, transportation, and the like are significant factors in many amateur pursuits. The more they scrimp on such matters as lessons, equipment, and repairs, the more their preparedness is diminished. And it is more difficult for amateur athletes than professionals, for instance, to justify spending scarce family funds on top-level sports equipment.

Self-Conception

It is evident from the Project that amateurs and professionals conceive of themselves in these very terms: as amateurs and professionals. Indeed, this sort of identification is still one of the most valid and practicable of operational measures. Nonetheless, the Projects did turn up additional information about the nature of their self-conceptions.

The principal observation was that established amateurs seldom saw themselves as inferior to their professional counterparts. To be sure, they recognized outstanding professionals in their fields who outshine everyone, amateurs and professionals alike. But, in terms of excellence, the ordinary professional was often seen as close to the good amateur. Usually, however, important qualifying conditions entered into these comparisons. For instance, many amateur stand-up comics said they could be as funny as professionals as long as both were allotted 20 minutes before a standard, comedy club, audience. Nevertheless, the amateurs did acknowledge that professionals have more prepared material from which to choose. Also, the professionals were believed to be better at controlling problematic audiences. Take amateur football players, who were convinced that they were as strong and quick, if not more so, as their professional colleagues, but who felt that the latter were more experienced at playing the positions.

The professionals, by the way, sometimes agreed with these assessments. Professional football players, for example, often admitted that it was their extensive experience that really separated them from good university players. Professional magicians, on the other hand, acknowledged the superior technical ability of some amateurs, while also commenting widely on their failure to entertain well. It was only in the science arena that a sharp distinction emerged between amateurs and professionals with respect to excellence. Yet, even here, in instances where amateurs collected data later used by professionals to test or develop theory, several professionals commented that amateurs can be as good at what they do. For their part, the amateurs sometimes distinguished themselves by commenting on the reluctance, even the inability, of the professionals to gather such data (in mycology, see Fine 1987, 234–6).

It is more difficult for early amateurs to distinguish themselves from dabblers in the same activity. Many of the amateurs I interviewed wondered early on in their careers when they could begin to think of themselves as true practitioners rather than mere neophytes. In other words, how accomplished or knowledgable must one be before daring to claim the identity of comic, musician, astronomer, or baseball player? I found that the answer to this question was always very personal, although certainly feedback from others as to the respondent's progress always entered the equation. In this connection, the receipt of a fee for one's amateur efforts, – something possible in all four fields – is symbolic of the attainment of a certain level of competence; it represents the point at which one can claim with some legitimacy to be a practitioner, a neophyte no longer (also see Finnegan 1989, 293).

These five attitudes together comprise a social, psychological definition of amateur. The assumption should be avoided that professionals hold them in ideal, or pure, form. That seldom happens. Indeed, even though professionals are significantly more confident, persevering, committed, and prepared than amateurs, they generally fall short of the highest points on these continua.

AMATEURS: ON THE MARGIN OF LEISURE

One major conclusion to be drawn from what has been said so far is that the amateurs of today, in all fields, and to the extent that they are guided by professional standards and share the same spirit of satisfaction, find themselves on the margin of modern leisure. They are neither dabblers who approach the activity with little commitment or seriousness, nor professionals who make a living from that activity, spending a major portion of their waking hours doing so, and for whom it is an occupation. Amateurs, as all eight studies demonstrated, thus fall somewhere along that continuum – possessing a constellation of properties unique to themselves. I suspect that research will eventually permit us to say the same for hobbyists and career volunteers.

One property of marginality, as incongruent as it may seem to the general public and some social scientists, is the degree to which commitment and leisure (Buchanan 1985; Shamir 1988), or investment of time and energy in a leisure role (Kelly 1983, 195–6), can coexist comfortably in the same sphere of activity. Lewis (1982), for example, overlooks the discretionary aspects of leisure when he argues that businessmen are really at work in their leisure. He also overlooks the fact that serious leisure will usually be enjoyable only if the level of considerable skill and knowledge demanded is approached and maintained. For example, it is much more enjoyable, and at the same time fulfilling, to play the piano well than to dabble at it. To accomplish the former, however, requires systematic practice – in a word, commitment or investment.

Another property of marginality is the seriousness with which amateurs approach their leisure. This seriousness leads, more often than not, to misunderstandings with friends, neighbours, relatives, and even spouses who, in the absence of serious pursuits, know leisure only as spectators, dabblers, or participants in casual pastimes. The seriousness of amateurs is evident in their orientation to their activities, in their talk about them, and, most significantly, in their willingness to work toward perfection. "No scientist, no doctor-fiddler," writes Catherine Drinker Bowen (1935, 68), "comes to quartets with strings broken from neglect or a bow stiff from lack of practice." Holtz (1977, 504) notes that both the public and the scientific community look on bridge as frivolous activity, unworthy of serious attention as leisure activity or scientific research: "The public stereotype of bridge among non-players, which includes most sociologists, as a superfluous pastime of middle-class suburbanites, exacerbates the stigma." Indeed, seriousness at leisure sets the modern amateur off from the majority of people, who find such an orientation foreign, possibly a bit quaint or snobbish and, more rarely, admirable.

Consider Andy Capp, the beloved idler of British cartoons with a strong penchant for billiards, who, after being shunned by his wife and insulted by the neighbours on his way to the billiard hall (stick over one shoulder), commented: "Marvelous, isn't it. If you're a pro an' play for money, they're askin' for your autograph. Play for the sheer joy of it an' you're a layabout. What's the matter with people?" Mind you, the amateurs interviewed in the Project never saw themselves as even "marginally deviant," as Goffman (1963, 143–5) has classified people who are exceptionally committed to an avocation. In effect, his term "the quietly disaffiliated" is probably not a bad description.

A third property of amateur marginality is the tendency toward uncontrollability. For instance, having spent the evening before observing stars or playing football, the amateurs in these studies often found themselves in a less than optimal working condition the next day. There is always, as well, the temptation to increase the time available for amateur interests by subtracting time from work, living, or non-work obligations. Indeed, a professional violinist used to counsel his daughter, "Rachel, never marry an amateur violinist! He will want to play quartets all night" (in Bowen 1935, 93). For those who find the small and occasional monetary rewards of amateurism attractive, this tendency is only exacerbated. Then there is the universal desire to upgrade: to own a better set of golf clubs, to buy a more powerful telescope, to take more dance lessons perhaps from a renowned (and consequently more expensive) professional, and so forth. In short, amateur activity stands ready to devour all the practitioners' time and money.

The tendency toward uncontrollability is likely found in various forms of casual leisure as well, should we look carefully. Implicit in that statement, however, is the hypothesis that uncontrollability is significantly greater among amateurs in all fields, particularly devotees, than among, for example, dabblers or spectators. Remember that many pastimes, no matter how unmanageable, are not really marginal, but are solidly entrenched as part of our leisure activities (e.g., evening television, social drinking).

A fourth property of the amateurs' marginality is linked to the fact that they can never gain complete entry to the professional world and still remain amateurs. Indeed, by their very lifestyle, amateurs are consigned to a peripheral role in the activity system of their "significant others," the professionals. Being peripheral in this way leads to feelings of inferiority. As an amateur mycologist put it: "To the amateur the [professional] mycologist is a hero and demigod, sorcerer and soothsayer, who brings to the foray an air of authority and to the obsession an air of responsibility. To the professional, the amateur is an ardent, sometimes tiresome proselyte whose votive offerings are viewed as fair exchange for instructing the uninitiated into the mysteries of nomenclature and identification (Friedman 1986, 99)." Among many amateurs the feelings of awe and inferiority seem to engender a level of gullibility: a propensity to accept unquestioningly any statement or judgment made by a respected professional about the activity.

Fifth is the sense of frustration that amateurs evince. That frustration comes from internalizing high standards of performance yet lacking sufficient time and possibly the experience, training, and equipment with which to meet those standards. Although amateurs try to keep their leisure aims to a manageable level, there are no specifically amateur or intermediate standards to serve as a guide. Nor will there ever be any, so long as high-level professional attainments (made possible by full-time striving) remain visible and dominant throughout the PAP system. Witness, too, the performance of a community orchestra, which is judged by such criteria as dynamics, intonation, and ensemble playing, just as is that of a professional orchestra. Critics have been known to observe that such performances are "pretty good *for a community orchestra*," which simply indicates that they have accepted, for the moment, a truncated expression of professional standards. At bottom, however, there is no double standard in sport, science, entertainment, or the arts. Today, products of or performances by amateurs and professionals alike are truly meritorious only to the extent that they approach perfection in these dimensions (in sport see Albinson 1976).[7]

CONCLUSIONS

This treatment of today's amateurs as the marginal people of leisure brings us full circle in our definition process. We noted, at the beginning, that two criteria distinguish professionals from amateurs. First, the former earn at least 50 percent of their livelihood from the focal activity, whereas the latter do not. Second, the former put in considerably more time at their activity than do the latter. Although these two truisms provide useful operational definitions for certain research questions, they do so only because they relate both amateurs and professionals to the underlying occupational, continuance commitment process – that is, professionals are committed to a certain pursuit and amateurs to a livelihood outside it.

But, as already noted, these definitions provide us with false leads for tracking down the essence of the late twentieth-century amateur. The foregoing discussion of marginality and the following chapters show us why that is so. Indeed, it seems that modern amateurs would like to spend more time and, at times, more money at their avocations than they have done in the past. My observations suggest, in fact, that many of them are in no way opposed to making money at their pursuits – even a lot of it – as long as their pursuits continue to be voluntary and enjoyable.

There were many reports throughout this Project of amateurs making small amounts of money at their serious leisure activities: quarterbacks throwing passing drill or pitchers throwing batting practice for a professional team; archaeologists consulting for government or industry on the antiquities buried beneath a future construction site; magicians and comics receiving small fees for performances (the former are expected to seek pay according to the norms of their art); and musicians filling in at union wages in a professional symphony orchestra. For the amateurs' families, the money helped to justify the practitioners' participation, while compensating for expenses and generally augmenting the family budget. At times, such earnings can even help to pay for the coveted items, mentioned earlier, that are sought by the amateurs. To repeat, it is the amateurs' very marginality that must eventually steer us from simplistic definitions to more complex ones, based on social organization and attitudinal differences.

As we proceed through this book, we must avoid the unidimensional thinking that pits amateur against professional in terms of, say, little versus great skill, intrinsic versus extrinsic reward, avocational versus vocational orientation, or leisure versus work activity. Although under certain conditions such dichotomies accurately describe the relationship, under many others they badly distort that relationship. The way to avoid this conceptual trap is to shift the theoretical perspective to a broader, more sociological definition of amateurs and professionals as members of PAP systems and as types with distinct attitudinal patterns. These dichotomies of skill, reward, and so on have been integrated into the new definitions. Indeed, the contradictions have been worked out to a substantial degree, and their tendency toward overgeneralization contained.

CHAPTER FOUR

Publics

In the sociology of occupations, we customarily think of people being served by professionals as "clients," as people interacting in personal service relationships with highly specialized practitioners. As noted in chapter 2, this conception does not dovetail with the sets of consumers who gather around the professionals in the arts, science, sport, and entertainment fields. In these areas, the dyadic link implied in the notion of client is comparatively rare. For instance, although painters and composers are occasionally commissioned by an individual or an organization to create a work, and scientists may consult or do contract work, this practice is unheard of among, say, writers, golfers, jugglers, instrumentalists, hockey players, and mime artists. Thus, in the PAP system, clients become *publics*: sets of people with a common interest; people not served by, but rather informed, enlightened, or entertained by professionals or amateurs, or both, and who make active demands upon them.

An important, although usually small, part of any public is made up of the amateurs and professionals themselves as they consume the products of their colleagues.[1] Since this complicated relationship was examined elsewhere, it will not be discussed in this chapter. Rather, I will concentrate largely on the *lay* as opposed to the *collegial* public, recognizing, however, that there is variation in the sophistication of the lay members. This variation is due, in part, to the fact that amateur publics are often composed substantially of friends and relatives of the amateurs. Indeed, the former may consume the amateurs' leisure products as much out of a sense of interpersonal obligation as out of a sense of appreciation.

Given the focus of the Project on amateurs and professionals, the publics of these two categories were never systematically studied. The only reason for this omission was the enormity of the task of studying, as a sole researcher, the various amateurs and professionals and their interrelationships. Nonetheless, the publics are an important part of any PAP system. From the beginning, I recognized that they were clearly related to the other two components of the system in at least five ways. First, they provide financial support for professionals, and sometimes, amateurs, in return for their products (e.g., by purchasing tickets, making donations). Second, they provide both groups with feedback as to the adequacy of those products (e.g., applause, compliments). Third, they thereby provide role-support (and sometimes non-support). Fourth, publics sometimes have an actual part in an amateur or professional production, as in dancing to or singing with live music (Finnegan 1989, 83 and 151). Finally, amateurs and professionals take the public's outlook and limitations into account when composing, constructing, or producing works. The eight studies add considerable detail to these five relationships.

FINANCIAL SUPPORT

It is obvious that professionals receive financial support from their publics. But what about amateurs who, both theoretically and stereotypically, are supposed to pursue their serious leisure for the pure love of it? Theory and stereotype aside, the Project provides ample evidence that a significant proportion of all amateurs, indeed, are directly or indirectly remunerated by some segment of their publics. We turn first to the domain of science.

Of the two sciences studied, only archaeology offered its amateurs the possibility of some sort of monetary return. Here master amateurs sometimes consult for government or industry on the scientific value of a future construction site. By way of surveys and other types of preliminary study, they can determine if anything of archaeological interest lies below the planned building or road. Local antiquity laws in North America typically provide for surveys and, if the surveys justify, for excavations before the site is forever obliterated in the name of development.

In sport, small financial gains accrue to, for example, amateur pitchers who are hired to pitch for the batting practices of professional teams. This arrangement conserves the "arms" of the professionals, which risk being overused. In professional Canadian and American football, a university quarterback may be hired for training camp simply to throw passes to the gang of players trying out for the position of receiver. In effect, there are too few quarterbacks on the typical professional team to fill this temporary need. In addition to these specialized instances of financial return, one finds clandestine payments being made in the industrial baseball leagues to valued pitchers and hitters. The company represented by the team is trying to enhance its commercial image through excellence in sport. Legitimate financial rewards are directly available from purses that go to the winners of pro-am contests in golf, tennis, and racketball and indirectly available to North American college and university athletes who win sports scholarships.

The financial support mentioned so far comes from special segments of the public: government, business, private sponsors, professional teams, and educational institutions. In art and entertainment, the general lay public may provide such support. Thus, amateur painters may occasionally sell a canvas, amateur writers an article, or amateur musicians their services as a member of a band or orchestra. Although these amateurs do not always command the same fee, or price, for their products as their professional counterparts, the money earned may still be considerable. Finally, in theatre, classical music, and possibly other fine arts, amateur groups receive donations from the public and support from governments and foundations to carry on their activities.

Of the four areas, public financial support is most pronounced among amateur entertainers. In the study of entertainment magic, I learned that amateurs are *expected* to charge a fee when they perform. Failure to do so, says the International Brotherhood of Magicians, results in systematic undercutting of the professional market. Only charitable bookings are excluded from this rule. The comedy study revealed that amateurs began to make minor amounts of money – fifteen dollars, a small percentage of the cover charge – only after they had developed into more or less consistently entertaining performers. At the time they were about to be "promoted" to professional status many were earning fifty dollars or so, on weekday evenings, as emcees or opening acts.

FEEDBACK

Feedback is the public's reaction to the products of the amateurs and professionals. In most fields of pure scientific research, feedback from the lay public is nil or diffuse. Usually, scientific findings are too specialized to have a direct impact, although we could consider the popularizations of science by a handful of scientists, notably David Suzuki and Isaac Asimov, as an important exception to this observation. However, even when members of the lay public read about scientific research in the popular press, or in such educational publications as *Science*, *Psychology Today*, and *New Statesman and Society*, their reactions are unlikely to reach the writer.

The picture is different, of course, on the level of applied science, which, because few amateurs are found there, is beyond the scope of this book. Certainly scientists are quick to learn of the public's reaction to a cure for cancer, an engineering marvel (e.g., the tunnel under the English channel), or another breakthrough in electronic gadgetry. But such innovation comes from those who are fully employed in established institutions, specially licensed (e.g., engineers, physicians), and in a position to patent and market new ideas.

Public reaction is generally direct and evident in the other three areas studied. The public provides feedback at sports events, for example, by cheering and booing, by writing letters to the editors of local newspapers, by buying or refusing to buy tickets, by seeking autographs or other social contact, and the like. Yet, feedback in the sports world falls, in terms of its importance, midway between the feedback in pure science and that in art and entertainment. In effect, the athletic contest itself is even more important than spectator opinion and social contact. A team can play a game of baseball, for example, with few or no fans in the stands (as many amateurs do) and still enjoy it immensely because of the inherent appeal of the sport. Feedback from fans is nice, if it is favourable, but hardly essential.

Such a stance does not hold, however, in art and entertainment. Artists create their product with the public in mind, as a form of communication. If the communication fails, the artistic product fails. When people fail to laugh, cry, marvel, tremble, or otherwise react in the way intended by the artists, the meaning of the work has clearly been lost. The absence of such reactions is, to be sure, a kind of feedback, but there is little to salvage in its wake. The contrast with the exciting game played before empty stands, or the intriguing stellar occultation observed alone on a cold winter's night, is only too clear.

Nonetheless, communication, an essential quality of art, does vary from art to art and entertainment to entertainment. Consider writers, for example. They receive feedback only belatedly in sales reports, book reviews, and requests for autographs. Painters are in more or less the same position. Stand-up comics, on the other hand, immediately know the impact of their lines when the audience laughs, groans, smiles, or remains expressionless. There appears to be no more obvious and direct feedback than that elicited by performed humour, whether presented in a play or a variety act.

A special kind of feedback comes from the journalistic critic: the person who evaluates in the mass media the products of those in art, sport, and entertainment. The public of these critics is the lay public of the amateurs and professionals. Thus, critics act as "audience mediators" (Truzzi 1978), particularly for PAP systems, where specialization has evolved to such a degree that the laity needs help in interpreting the nature and quality of artistic and athletic efforts.

It is no secret that journalistic critics are frequently scorned by artists, athletes, and entertainers (Lacroix 1990, 190–3), although Simpson (1989, 58) observes that critical appraisals of the latter, because their acts present little conceptual challenge, turn out to be chiefly previews. Mark Twain observed that the "trade of critic in literature, music, and the drama is the most degraded of all trades." Disraeli saw critics as failures in art and literature. Gustave Flaubert said "One becomes a critic when one cannot become an artist, just as a man becomes a stool pigeon when he cannot be a soldier" (in painting, see Rosenberg and Fliegel 1965, 209–10). As for the sports analyst, the equivalent in the sports world, the football players, though less poetic, were no more complimentary. But perhaps there is good reason, if this sportswriter's remarks, made in 1938 about baseball rookie Ted Williams, are any indication: "I don't like the way he stands at the plate. He bends his front knee inward and moves his foot just before he takes a swing. That's exactly what I do before I drive a golf ball and knowing what happens to the golf balls I drive, I don't believe this kid will ever hit half a singer midget's weight in a bathing suit" (quoted in Cerf and Navasky 1984, 194).

Just the same, the amateurs and professionals interviewed in these studies were clearly pleased when a critic commented favourably on their efforts. Hanna (1988, 34–8) and Crane (1989, 268–9) have reported that dance and art critics are sometimes seen as sources of important evaluation, especially for new dances. In reality, it is probably most accurate to say that a love-hate relationship exists in this area of the PAP system, although much less for amateurs than professionals, for the former invariably lament the tendency of the mass media to ignore them altogether.[2] My observations indicate, further, that on the rare occasion that an amateur product is considered in the press, the treatment is largely descriptive. What evaluation there is is likely to be charitable.

ROLE SUPPORT

Simply put, role support constitutes encouragement of any sort that motivates participants to continue their pursuits. When positive, feedback is a form of role support, as is some of the financial support mentioned earlier. The concept of role support serves to underscore the fact that the lay public (not to mention the collegial public) is an important motivating force in the PAP system. From what was said in the preceding section, it follows that this force is strongest in the areas of art and entertainment, moderately strong in sport, and weakest in science.

One segment of the lay public that has a large part to play in supporting practitioners in art, sport, and entertainment is their close friends and relatives. Many an athlete, thespian, musician, (Finnegan 1989, chapter 15), magician, and stand-up comic warmly acknowledged the behind-the-scenes encouragement received over the years from "significant others" of every kind. In other words, role support is more than the motivational jolt of positive feedback given in response to a particular performance or production. It is also the day-to-day prodding to work harder, refuse to give up, ignore unjust criticism, and persevere in the face of favouritism. This small set of supportive people also helps to celebrate success and interpret bad breaks; they are present for all or a substantial part of the practitioner's leisure or work career, unlike the rest of the lay public with whom contact is sporadic and ephemeral. We shall return to the role of supporters in chapter 7.

PUBLIC PARTICIPATION

As mentioned earlier, public participation in the productions of professionals and amateurs is limited to the fields of art and entertainment. Of course, one might ask if the human subjects used in scientific research are not a special public, but that falls outside our definition. Subjects are not sets of people with a common interest who are informed by the scientists. Rather the first are exploited by the second for the purpose of obtaining or generating scientific information. Similarly, in sport, the different publics play no direct role in the athletic contests they have come to watch.

Fine artists are much less likely than entertainers to incorporate the public in a production or work. Still, Noble (1970) found instances of such incorporation in musical compositions by Malcolm Arnold and Benjamin Britten, among others. Naturally, commissioned works in painting, sculpting, music (Faulkner 1976; Stebbins 1969), photography (Christopherson 1974, 134–5), and the crafts may be influenced to some extent by the wishes or tastes of the buyer.

I found the highest level of public participation in productions in the field of entertainment. Here stand-up comics banter with members of the audience; magicians invite "volunteers" onstage to assist with a trick; and singing groups call on the audience to clap in rhythm or sing the refrain of a song. In New Orleans, black marching bands mingle with their audiences as musicians and listeners alike strut and dance to jazzlike tunes. Consider the participation found in total theatre:

Get the audience involved. The new gimmick is entitled "total theatre." A group of youngsters have introduced it in London's Tara-Hotel.

What they do is to stage a play, *Another Bride, Another Groom*, a comedy about a wedding reception. The play is acted out in the hotel's banquet room, and the audience is invited to eat and drink as wedding guests. They join in toasts, sing songs, and end up dancing with members of the cast, one of whom, Seretta Wilson, who plays a bridesmaid, delights the audience with a revealing striptease.

Says director Eleanor Fazan: "We experimented with a theatre-restaurant production in Melbourne, Australia, where it was boozy and ribald and wonderful. In London, it's been equally successful. Now we're thinking of bringing it to the United States. (*Parade*, 1975, 16)

In all these examples, the public is an integral part of the production and, thus, an indispensable element in the PAP system.

Unwanted public participation sometimes occurs as well. One form is heckling, the bane of many stand-up comics, folk performers (Sanders 1974, 276), night club musicians and gogo dancers (Mullen 1985). The spontaneous blurting of remarks or observations about the performer's material, what comics refer to as "calling out," is related to heckling. Although the remarks are not insulting, as they are in heckling, they nonetheless interrupt the comic's line of ideas that carries listeners along toward the punchline of a joke. As disagreeable as unwanted public participation is for entertainers, it is still part of the PAP system; indeed, heckling and calling out constitute distinct kinds of social relations between entertainers and their audiences.

PUBLIC LIMITATIONS

The term "public limitations" delineates the public's capacity to understand and appreciate an amateur-professional production. Such limitations are a central concern in applied science as well, where human beings are often served directly. Feedback from the public reflects what scientists know and do not know about the limitations of the laity. Examples of the results of such lacks of knowledge are all too familiar: building designs that frustrate legitimate uses of space, computer programs that are not user-friendly, and automotive designs that annoy.

Of the four areas of amateur-professional endeavour studied, I found public limitations to be of least concern in the domain of sport. Even there, however, one finds modifications designed to enhance fan appeal and, in the end, ticket sales or television receipts (Altheide and Snow 1979, 228). Take, for instance, the rule in professional basketball that forces the team with possession of the ball to shoot within twenty-four seconds, or the one in American and Canadian football that limits the amount of time that can be spent in the huddle.

It is in the worlds of art and entertainment, however, that public limitations figure most prominently in the productions of practitioners. As already mentioned, the artists (both fine and popular) in these areas are trying to communicate with their public. My studies demonstrate how important it is for the artists to be able to take into account the role of this public if they are to communicate effectively. The artists must be able to see how members of the public regard their artistic work (Collingwood 1958, 314). But does the public have the knowledge or background to understand that work and react as the artist intended? As French artist Paul Valéry put it: "The painter should not paint what he sees, but what will be seen."

Magicians know that their physical and mental anomalies must be familiar to their audiences if their acts are to succeed as entertainment, as wonderment. Randi (1978, 56) reports that although the Shipibo Indians of Peru were not at all impressed with a handkerchief that changed colours, they were astounded when a stone was made to disappear. Whereas the second was a real and familiar object, the first was something they had never before seen. As for stand-up comics, they must present monologues about familiar subjects and in such a way that their audience is amused. That requires a deep sense of what is humorously incongruent in everyday life. It was Gans (1962) who studied how Hollywood film producers take public limitations into account in their productions.

CONCLUSIONS

The importance of the public in the PAP system looms ever larger when a particular professional-amateur pursuit lacks an intrinsic, self-contained quality. Interestingly, sport has this quality, as does science to some extent: the first invokes the pleasure of a contest; the second, the interest of a puzzle. Lay publics can be ignored in the course of realizing these private benefits, although collegial publics usually cannot.

The public is clearly more indispensable in the arts and entertainment fields. Whether in reality or imagination, the publics, lay and collegial, are present at every step in the production of each art and entertainment form; indeed, they constitute an integral part of it all. However one conceives of the amateurs and professionals in these areas (as stars, gurus, pacesetters), the public plays a role in the PAP system that knows no equivalent in sport and science.

In an age in which there is a marked tendency to glamorize the seemingly smooth, proficient, super competent professional (and elite amateur), it is good to remember the importance of the public. To overlook the public, bedazzled by the performers, on whom the spotlight consistently plays, is to overlook the essence of any system; namely, its interdependent parts, its mutual cause and effect links, and its historical and organizational foundation. Rosenberg and Fliegel (1970, 499) found in their study that painters hold mixed sentiments about their publics. On the one hand, the artists believed they painted out of inner necessity and not in response to public influences. Yet, they also hoped that their works would serve some wider purpose; at bottom, they hoped their works would be seen by people able to grasp the message that each work was intended to communicate. Thus Rosenberg and Fliegel found, for painters, what is true for many amateur-professional participants: an audience or public is essential. Or as Erwin Piscator (1949, 286) observed: "There is no theatre without an audience."

This brings us to the final point to be made in this chapter, a point that bears on PAP systems in general; namely, that professionals, amateurs, and their publics actually coalesce into *core* systems of relations and relationships. For example, paralleling the development of any PAP system is the development of a range of auxiliary functions that must materialize in order to facilitate the production or consumption of a particular art, science, sport, or entertainment. For example, the aforementioned critic performs an auxiliary function. Other such individuals are the teachers, publishers, trainers, librarians, impresarios, booking agents, museum curators, stage crews, art dealers, and equipment suppliers and repairers. Individuals working at institutions, such as foundries, laboratories, recording studios, and marketing agencies, should be mentioned here as well.

These roles have been variously conceptualized in the social scientific literature, usually, however, with reference only to the fine or popular arts. There Truzzi (1978) refers to them as "mediators," and Becker (1982, ch. 3) calls them "resources." Suffice to say, here, that since this book is about PAP systems and not their auxiliary functions, the people performing these functions are, themselves, often highly skilled, even professional. Moreover, most practitioners become heavily dependent on a number of them, even if it is possible, in principle, to pursue the central activity without them. Finally, as Becker (1982, 70) has noted for the fine arts, the people performing these functions have their own preferences and requirements that can affect the PAP system, sometimes profoundly. All this means that the auxiliary functions must be included in any complete analysis of a given art, science, sport, or entertainment, even if I have largely ignored them here in this narrower study of amateurs, professionals, and publics.

CHAPTER FIVE

Careers

As indicated in chapter 1, the notion of a career is itself an important concept in the study of serious leisure; it goes without saying that the concept is equally important in the study of professional work. Indeed, in art, science, sport, and entertainment, the idea of a career acts as a major bridge between amateur and professional activity. It has, moreover, the capacity to link individual amateurs or professionals (or other workers) with the culture and social structure within which the work and leisure activities are pursued. For example, some careers take their incumbent through a series of organizational positions. Others vault a popular artist or athlete into the limelight, illuminating this person in the popular culture of the day. Thus, a career can also serve as a bridge between the microsociological and macrosociological, as well as the static and dynamic, areas of life. One takes as a given, here, the fact that personal status changes can occur within more or less fixed sets of organizational or cultural arrangements, or both.

The definition of a career that has evolved over the fifteen years of this Project is uniquely suited to the situation of amateurs and professionals in these four areas. Simply put: a career is the typical course, or passage, of certain types of amateur-professional practitioners that carries them into, and through, a leisure role and possibly into, and through, a work role. The essence of a career lies in the temporal continuity of the activities associated with it. We are accustomed to thinking of this continuity as one of accumulating rewards and prestige, as progress along these lines from some starting point. But continuity may also include career retrogression. In the world of sport and entertainment, for instance, athletes and artists may reach performance peaks early on, after which the prestige and rewards diminish as the limelight shifts to younger, sometimes more capable, practitioners.

Continuity in the work careers of people may occur predominantly within, between, or outside organizations. Careers in organizations such as the military, government, or business commonly unfold as workers move up through a hierarchy of positions or ranks, each offering the incumbent more attractive rewards and prestige. Downward mobility, though rarer, also takes place.

Amateurs and professionals in the art, science, sport, and entertainment areas typically have careers across two or more organizations. That is, these professionals are independent professionals. For them, career continuity stems from their growing reputations as skilled, knowledgable practitioners and, based on this image, from finding increasingly better work and pay opportunities available through a variety of outlets (such as teams, orchestras, tournaments, exhibitions, journals, conferences, contests, shows, and the like). Although some professionals belong to small-scale organizations (such as teams, companies, orchestras, and clubs), their careers usually develop as they move from one to another. Other professionals who pursue a non-collective line of work (e.g., tennis, painting, magic, clowning, golf) are free of even this marginal affiliation with a work organization.

In short, the continuity of the career of a public-centred professional is similar to that of many independent physicians, lawyers, consultants, small business people, and university professors. It is substantially different, however, from that of most police officers, civil servants, corporation managers, military personnel, and clergy in the Anglican and Roman Catholic churches.

Career continuity can be viewed from two perspectives: a) from the *career history*, or the chronological, descriptive, objective view of the career as it unfolds over the active years of the typical amateur and professional; or b) from the *subjective career*; or the career as seen through the eyes of the people pursuing it. In effect, the subjective career focuses on the incumbents' interpretation of what has happened, is happening, and will likely happen to them at various times during their lives as practitioners of the central activity.

THE CAREER FRAMEWORK

In sociology, career histories are commonly explored from the standpoint of a progression of stages through which the incumbent passes. As far as the study of amateurs and public-centred professionals is concerned, none of the conventional category progressions is wholly adequate (e.g., Super 1957; Miller and Form 1980). To meet this deficiency, I developed the following sequence – basically a hybrid of the established progressions and the distinct careers of those in the four amateur-professional areas over the course of the Project; that sequence involves five stages of progression: a beginning, development, establishment, maintenance, and decline. The first two are strictly amateur stages; the last three are shared by both amateurs and professionals. Because some pure amateurs choose to continue their serious leisure at a high level of involvement until retirement or decline, both categories of practitioners can be found in the latter three stages. Fine artists, avocational scientists, and elite amateur athletes are found in this group. One cautionary note: these stages are far from precise; each overlies the other to a degree.

At each stage in their career history, practitioners encounter special contingencies. A *career contingency* is an unintended event, process, or situation that occurs by chance; that is, it lies beyond the control of the people pursuing the career. Career contingencies emanate from changes in leisure or work environments or personal circumstances, or both. Thus the movement of people, whether progressive or retrogressive, through careers is affected by the contingencies they meet along the way.

The idea of a subjective career refers to the practitioner's recognition and interpretation of the events – past, present, and future – associated with his or her work or leisure role (Stebbins 1970a). Especially important in any analysis of the subjective side of a career is the practitioners' interpretation of the turning points already encountered or expected. It is from a description of their subjective careers that we learn how amateurs and professionals have determined continuity in their work and leisure lives – how they see themselves as progressing or declining.

A *turning point* is a juncture at which the nature or direction of an amateur-professional career is seen by the practitioners as having changed significantly. In general, the turning points in a career are the critical events and decisions experienced and made in the course of the work or leisure. Certain career contingencies may be interpreted as turning points; for example, getting injured in a game or discovering a comet. Other important events such as winning an award, succeeding at an audition, and deciding on a specialty, while not contingent, are still seen as turning points. They fail to qualify as contingencies because, to a significant degree, they are caused and controlled by the practitioners themselves. Some turning points, then, are contingent; some are not.

The remainder of this chapter encapsulates what I learned about amateurs and professionals as they progressed through the five stages of their career histories, interpreting the contingencies and turning points as they went. The emphasis in the early stages is on *career entry*; the combination of contingencies and turning points that funnel the practitioners, often unconsciously, toward the amateur-professional pursuit. I have eschewed the idea of recruitment here, for it refers rather narrowly to "the process of screening, wooing, and eliminating before the career actually starts" (Glaser 1968, 56). As mentioned earlier, recruitment is possible in certain, usually client-centred professions, because the practitioners have the power to admit whom they wish. This is not the case, however, with the public-centred professions, which is why recruitment, as just defined, is an inadequate concept around which to organize a treatment of the amateur professional career.

THE BEGINNING

The beginning of the amateur-professional career lasts as long as is necessary for interest in the activity to take root. This is clearly a stage with imprecise boundaries, for some amateurs develop their interest only gradually, whereas others are struck by it suddenly, on the spot as it were. But even "love at first sight" does not always mean an automatic whisking to the next stage of a career. Rather, neophytes usually need to mobilize in some way, so they can pursue the activity on a more or less regular basis and as something they would now definitely like to do, improve at, be seen in, and so on.

Technically, one is not even an amateur at this point, for one of the main career contingencies lies in developing a substantial awareness of the pursuit itself. This may happen either abruptly or gradually. For many artists, both fine and popular, there is a memorable, abrupt contact with their art that launches them into a career. Agnes de Mille describes her entry into dance: "It was only after seeing the matinee performance of Adeline Genée, dainty, doll-like and impeccable, that I altered my choice of vocation. I declared on coming home that henceforth I would be a ballet dancer, and that Mother might arrange about lessons for the next day. There were, however, no lessons, but nevertheless I danced" (de Mille, 1952, 3). Interviews with painters and poets convey the impact of major works on their decisions to devote their lives to their art, although they fall short of supporting André Malraux's sweeping conviction that every great artist traces his vocational interest to his reactions to a specific artistic work (Rosenberg and Fliegel 1965, 116–7; Wilson 1964, 25). For example, Teresa Wright saw Helen Hayes in *Victoria Regina*, an event she said "shaped her life." As well, Sandy Denois decided to become an actress after seeing Kim Stanley in a play (reported in Levy 1989, 121). Her evaluation was similar to that of a number of stand-up comics: the first time they saw live comedy it looked easy. It occurred to them that they could be even funnier than some of the people onstage and, in their naïvety, they were inspired to try their hand at it. A number of the comics related how they had developed a taste for their art from televised or recorded comedy, a grounding, they say, that put them in a receptive yet critical mood for their eventual first "live" contact with the comedy form.

Magicians are cut from the same cloth. Of the three ways of becoming interested in magic – doing it, reading about it, and seeing it done – the large majority of both professionals and amateurs trace their initial interest to the third: a live or televised performance of magic. The remainder of both samples got their start in magic from reading a book or magazine article, acquiring a magic set, or buying or receiving one or two separate tricks (see also Nardi 1983, 7). Some of those whose interest was piqued by a live performance had also been in the midst of reading about magic; some were even trying to work a trick or two.

A similar picture was found in astronomy. About two-thirds of the practitioners who became interested in their youth said their interest had been piqued during a memorable observation of some aspect of the nighttime sky and in the company of one or more special individuals, perhaps a father, brother, childhood friend (often one in the Scouting movement), or an adult neighbour or acquaintance (in microscopy, see Bowser 1978, 66). The remainder discovered astronomy through books which, naturally, was a solitary process. Whereas their first significant observation of the heavens, if it occurred at all, occurred later, those who started with observation invariably supplemented this with a substantial amount of reading. A large proportion of both amateurs and professionals mentioned an avid interest in reading about astronomy and other sciences. Whether one observes or reads during the beginning stage is partly related to the availability of a suitable observing instrument (telescope, binoculars). Those who observed with a scope – typically a commercial refractor with a two- to three-inch lens – were usually assisted by someone experienced in its use.

Most athletic careers, in contrast, have a gradual beginning somewhat along the following lines. While playing pickup football, baseball and other childhood sports, youngsters gain considerable satisfaction from the expression of athletic interests or from the admiration of others, both adults and peers; they may be intrigued by the nature of sports as well. During this early period, they discover their aptitude for sport; by pitting their skills against their peers, these youngsters learn whether they excel in physical activities (see also Kenyon and McPherson 1981, 224; Andrews 1981). For instance, all respondents in the football study said football was only one of several athletic interests developed at this stage. Even in high school (during the development stage), all but a few had played at least one sport, and usually two or three, in addition to football.

In sum, in the areas of art, science, and entertainment, the practitioners' start can be abrupt, springing from an initial, impressive, direct contact with the activity. Indirect contact, through books, records, magazines, and television, however, usually leads to a more gradual commencement; it can also serve to intensify the effect of the first direct contact. Such are the beginnings made in childhood or adolescence, when many athletes and fine artists get their start. Most scientists, by contrast, enter their careers as adults, after developing a broad interest in general science in school. Fields like theatre, writing, and stand-up comedy, perhaps because they rest on linguistic and interpretive skills which are perfected only in adulthood, generally attract enthusiasts no earlier than late adolescence. Nevertheless, a bookstore in Calgary is home to a club and workshop for writers 10 to 18 years of age (Zimmerman 1982, G8).

Late-blooming interests are more likely to develop independently of peers, family, and neighbours, as opposed to those acquired during childhood, which are frequently mediated by such people. The intimate social milieu is important. It imbues the future amateur, possibly professional, activity with an aura of friendliness, encouragement, and legitimacy. These others, if they are adults, may be in a position to supply the equipment (e.g., the first magic set or telescope) or arrange for the beginner to experience the activity directly, as in a show, concert, or exposition. In magic, perhaps some of the sciences, and in much of sport, childhood friends often provide the first contact with the activity and the first encouragement to try one's hand.

In a number of fields, parental approval can be a major contingency affecting passage to the career stage of development. In football, for example, parents must sign consent forms that permit their sons to play on organized teams. A minority of parents in my study were reluctant to sign; they believed the game was too rough or, especially among immigrants, too trivial. In several other pursuits, an adult, typically a parent, must provide money for equipment, lessons, memberships, and the like. Their understanding of the activity as being somehow valuable and appropriate for their son or daughter is clearly critical. As we shall see shortly, such approval is sometimes evanescent, reflecting parental definitions that the activity is suitable for their children only at a certain stage of development.

This last point leads us to the contingency of gender which, it turns out, operates at all stages of amateur-professional careers. In the beginning, it acts as a sort of sieve, filtering out males and females from activities culturally defined as appropriate for one sex only. Thus,

Nardi (1988, 764–6) found that entertainment magic is traditionally seen as the proper undertaking of males, because of the power, control, and competitive manipulation of others believed to be inherent to the art. By contrast, males have to contend with the public view that ballet dancing, and to a lesser degree theatre, are only for females (Perreault 1988; Levy 1989, 126). The stereotypes of the gender appropriate sports are particularly well known (Hart 1981, 452); as in, for example, hockey and football for males (involving strength and speed) and diving and ice skating for women (involving poise and rhythmic movement). As well known (e.g., Robinson and Salamon 1987, 130) is the observation that schools tend to foster the view that science, among other areas, is a boys' subject.

DEVELOPMENT

Development begins when interest in an activity takes root and its pursuit becomes systematic and routine. To be sure, personal improvement in an amateur-professional field lasts only as long as the practitioner stays in it. There is an infinite amount to be learned, experienced, or acquired; even those acknowledged to be the best are still developing in this sense. As a career stage, however, development ends, often gradually, when practitioners see themselves as having reached a point at which they can perform their specialty within the field with relative ease, where they no longer see themselves as learners or students. Passage through development to career establishment is achieved by many amateurs and all professionals.

It was in the study of stand-up comics that I finally found a way to conceptualize, in general terms, the process of development in amateur-professional careers. The scheme that emerged there, generalizable to all four areas, consists of five patterns of development. In the *sporadic* pattern the practitioner, rather like the dabbler, participates irregularly in the activity. In the *gradual* pattern, involvement becomes more and more frequent until it reaches a certain level of regularity, at which point the practitioner enters the *steady* pattern of development. Some of those in this last pattern face a need from time to time to interrupt their pursuit of the avocation, say, to work or attend school. They have a *broken-steady* pattern of development. Finally, the *delayed-steady* pattern is found among those practitioners who abandon their avocation for several months early in the development stage, but return to steady involvement later on.

The steady pattern was most common in stand-up comedy, where amateurs performed regularly during weekly "open-mike" nights after their initial appearance onstage, usually at a similar occasion.

Sporadic, broken-steady, and delayed-steady patterns were reported by smaller numbers of comics. The two sports studies, in contrast, suggested that sporadic involvement is most prevalent among youth, and that it holds until they join a team or start taking lessons, as in, for example, golf, tennis, or swimming. At this time they begin to participate steadily.

Careers at the development stage in the fine arts generally resemble those in sport at that point. Whether initial contact with an art is abrupt or gradual, early development is likely to be sporadic. Only when the neophyte enters some sort of formal training program does development proceed more steadily. Delayed and broken patterns appear to be less common here than in stand-up comedy or the other entertainment fields that attract mainly adults. For example, art and sport often attract children whose pursuit of the activity is unlikely to be interrupted by a competing interest (unless it is another budding avocation).

The dominant pattern of development in science falls between that found in art and sport and that found in entertainment, at least among adults. Children and adolescents who enter avocational science appear to follow a pattern undertaken by only a minority entering art and sport. Instead of being sporadically involved, they become gradually involved. The gradual introduction of more science in school probably accounts for this pattern, which holds until the teenager joins a science club or selects a particular science as a university major. At that time, pursuit becomes steady.

Still, the nature of some avocational science is such that development reaches a point where it becomes sporadic, or at least seasonal. Unlike much of art, sport, and entertainment, there are few skills in science, if any, that must be acquired and assiduously maintained through practice. Amateurs can observe stars, for example, when the temperature is comfortable; they can also be forced into inactivity because of a week of cloud or haze. Nevertheless, although northern ornithologists, archaeologists, and minerologists must wait for spring to resume pursuit of their avocations, some will still chose to collect data intermittently rather than steadily even in the spring, summer, and fall.

Contingencies

There are also numerous career contingencies in the development stage. Joining a team, starting lessons, or entering a club, at least for minors – all require parental, moral, and financial support. To a significant degree, such support lies beyond the neophyte's control. The availability of appropriate teams, clubs, and lessons is also a contingency. For example, there are no football teams in Newfoundland; in certain fine arts, towns and small cities may lack qualified instructors; and science clubs can be scarce outside the larger centres. Often, too, children serious about a career in ballet must attend a special school in a faraway city (Sutherland 1985, 102–3). When the opportunity *is* available, however, inasmuch as it definitely has potential for changing the direction of the practitioner's career, this last contingency can actually become a contingent turning point. Another contingent turning point encountered at this time is the quality of the instruction available through coaching and private lessons.

Underlying these contingencies is still another: the access of would-be participants to credible information about the organizations providing the leisure (Fine 1989). Boys, for example, must learn about the series of age-graded recreational leagues available in hockey, baseball, and football throughout much of North America. The football players I studied had not always had this knowledge in their younger days.

As well, physical limitations may become contingencies, from the development stage on. For example, however appealing the thought, aspirants may lack the manual dexterity to play, even passably, the piano or violin. And neophytes may not have the sense of balance required for ballet, the size to play line in football, the agility to succeed at basketball. Remember, too, that women are more likely than men to do the leg banding required in some ornithological research; their smaller hands and more delicate touch better equip them for the task.

A more nebulous contingency at this career stage may involve finding opportunities to talk with professionals. Amateurs at all career stages enjoy rubbing elbows with their full-time counterparts, so long as the occasion is free of insults, snubs, condescension, and similar unpleasantnesses. At the development stage, salutary contact, because of its rarity, can be especially motivating. Professionals represent the highest expression of the activity that beginning amateurs dream of mastering. Chance encounters with such people can be inspiring; the amateur may run into a magnetic personality or see, at close range, a dazzling demonstration of technique or knowledge. In addition, accounts of a profession and its stars may give the amateur a sense of being on the inside. Such encounters are also useful for amateurs who want to boast of their glamourous associations to associates inside or outside the field.

Making Progress

The neophyte becomes a true amateur during the development stage of the amateur-professional career and may advance far enough to reach the level of development found at the establishment stage. Each of the four areas has a distinct pathway of progress through development that is experienced as a subjective career. We turn first to art.

In general, progress during the development stage in art is manifested by the participant's growth of knowledge and ability – whether as a painter, musician, thespian, dancer, or writer – acquired through a combination of expert instruction, personal practice, and experience with public displays of one's art. The budding artist is taught, practises what he or she has learned, is evaluated, internalizes the evaluations, presents the art publicly, and is further evaluated. It is hoped that such a cycle brings about the requisite progress. Even in the amateur stage of development, there is, for the steadily improving practitioner, a more or less ascending set of prestigious opportunities to display one's artistic talents: exhibitions, recitals, competitions, and festivals, all organized by a range of sponsors (municipalities, conservatories, private teachers, public schools, charitable foundations).

In group-based arts, such as dance, theatre, and orchestral music, limited career progress is also possible through local advancement via a quasi-formal hierarchy. The improving violinist, for example, moves from section player to concertmaster or concertmistress in the university orchestra. The developing high school actress wins the lead in the class play. Groups may advance collectively as well, as in the youthful jazz band that finds increasingly better paying gigs, in more and more prestigious locations, for more and more refined audiences.

Sport is close to the fine arts in its pathway of progress through the development stage. Here, however, progress is measured in terms of growing skill, gained from the combination of solitary practice, coaching or private instruction, and experience in competing against others. Formal knowledge is less important in sport than in fine art, where theories as to how to create art emerge and often compete. Their nearest equivalent in sport may be the strategies used for trying to defeat competitors.

In amateur sport, as in art, there are ascending sets of prestigious opportunities for displaying talent: hierarchies of tournaments, leagues composed of club or school teams, meets, or competitions. Likewise, players can advance from reserve status to that of starter and, if exceptional, on to award winner (e.g., most valuable player, player of the week, member of the all-star team). Progress to this point in art and sport is much less contingent than it was in the beginning (although it is never wholly non-contingent). Now the artist's or player's own excellence is a major force in the career passage. Now there are turning points endowed with personal interpretations.

Because they almost always work alone, scientists and entertainers, when compared with artists and athletes, share some common ground in the way they move through the development stage. Both may be characterized as *amateur-professional entrepreneurs*. These entrepreneurs turn up in such pursuits as golf, running, painting, sculpting, astronomy, archaeology, entomology, entertainment, creative writing, magic shows, singles tennis, and stand-up comedy. Other amateurs line up under what might be loosely called *avocational collectivism*. They are found in dance, football, baseball, hockey, theatre, symphonic music, Broadway musicals, commercial dance music, and similar undertakings.

The differences between the entrepreneur and the collectivist in amateur-professional pursuits are manifested in the four dimensions of initiative, originality, independence, and risk. We turn, first, to these dimensions in entertainment, where entrepreneurship requires exceptional *initiative* to develop, promote, and perform an act in the highly competitive world of show business. Collective forms of entertainment, for example, professional hockey, commercial dance music, Broadway musicals, and dinner theatre, deny their practitioners the opportunity to express self-reliance in this manner.

Originality must accompany initiative if the artist is to succeed as an entertainer. The act must have a novel twist to attract an audience and hold its attention. To be sure, originality is sometimes evident in some of the collective activities just mentioned, but it is less frequent there than in the variety arts. It is one thing to be asked to play an occasional spirited solo as a member of an orchestra and quite another to do this regularly. If the audience is bored, an employer will refuse to book the comic in the future; meanwhile, the audience will spread the word about the performer's inadequacies. In contrast, the "off-form" performance of a Broadway singer or actor on a particular night is hidden, to some extent, in the overall performance of the group.

As entrepreneurs, variety artists also have a considerable measure of *independence* in managing their affairs, once under way. Compare their situation with that of performers who must follow the dictates of a coach, conductor, or director. As well, variety artists assume *risks* to a degree unknown in collective entertainment. For example, stand-up comics promoted to opening spots seldom sign a contract with an agent that guarantees sufficient work to justify quitting their day jobs. Entertainment entrepreneurs do not necessarily invest more time, energy (emotional, physical), and money in their pursuits than others, but they do risk failure more often. Conversely, success is theirs and theirs alone, for they initiate and guide their interests without significant aid or support from others.

Scientists are entrepreneurs in much the same way. That is, they initiate their own research problems and the studies designed to solve them. Although replications are welcome in science, the overall emphasis is firmly on original contributions, on new data, theory, and research methods. In carrying out projects, scientists typically have a great deal of independence, an observation that is largely invalid, however, for research assistants and full-fledged scientists working in totalitarian circumstances. Finally, scientists, much like entertainers, assume risks. They court both success and failure. Indeed, the project may turn out well and advance knowledge in the discipline, or it may turn out poorly – the product of weak design, untenable hypotheses, or unforeseen circumstances.[1]

The amateur-professional entrepreneur gets started in the development stage of a career. But the entrepreneurial nature of the career continues and, indeed, is subject to enhancement through increased knowledge about, and experience with, the ways and means of taking initiative, being original, developing independence, and reducing risk. As described here, entrepreneurship is, in fact, a powerful magnet pulling amateurs and professionals alike to science, entertainment, and the individual arts.

The entrepreneurial aspect of the amateur's life in art and entertainment does sometimes have a monetary element associated with it. During the development stage, this element is, in one sense, minor; amateurs make a living elsewhere – from a job, not from an avocation whose remuneration is minuscule. But, in another sense, the first paid expression of their art is very important – a major turning point at this time in their career.

There are at least four reasons for this interpretation. The first one was mentioned in chapter 3: a fee symbolizes the attainment of a certain level of competence; it allows the amateur to claim to be a genuine practitioner rather than a mere neophyte. Second, the fact that someone is willing to pay for the amateur's creation is evidence of its value to others. It suggests, however tentatively, that one's talents and abilities have a certain level of public appeal. Third, it represents the first experience with a formal, contractual arrangement with a consumer or group of consumers in the area of one's art. When money changes hands, expectations change as well. Because of this payment, the artist is expected to produce what the consumer wants, on time, and at the agreed-upon fee. Fourth, the first paid performance may be the artist's first public performance, earlier ones having been given informally before friends or relatives. Developing entertainers find themselves in settings where the professionals in the field operate: at recording and television studios, in auditoriums, on stages, or anywhere before an audience that is expecting a performance. In such situations, the level of perfection expected is generally higher than that expected in informal settings.

Types of Avocational Scientists

Before turning to the next stage of the amateur-professional career, let us examine the four types of avocational scientists. As will become apparent shortly, three fall along the continuum that depicts the scientific career at the amateur level, starting in development.

Drawing on a distinction used by amateur astronomers, it is possible to categorize all avocational scientists as either *observers* or *armchair participants*. The observers directly experience their objects of scientific inquiry; the armchair participants pursue their avocation largely, if not wholly, through reading. The latter hold to their approach either because they prefer it to observation or because they lack the time, equipment, opportunities, or physical stamina to go into their field or laboratory.

Amateurs vary much more than their professional counterparts in terms of their level of knowledge and degree of willingness and ability to contribute original data to their science. The observers can be classified according to one of three subtypes: apprentices, journeymen, or masters.[2] Scientific *apprentices* are learners. They hope to learn enough about their discipline, its research procedures, and its instrumentation so they can function as journeymen and eventually, perhaps, as masters. As their knowledge about science grows, apprentices may select a specialty, becoming learners here as well. Scientific apprentices, unlike their opposite number in the trades, are normally independent; formal association with a master over a prescribed period of time is nonexistent. Even at this stage, individuals have the freedom of an avocational entrepreneur, although, typically, they are incapable of contributing anything original to their field. Archaeology is an exception; its apprentices must be supervised lest they do irreparable damage to a site.

Journeymen are knowledgable, reliable practitioners who can work independently in one or a few specialties. They have advanced far enough to make original contributions to the science in question. It is a matter of self-definition, however, as to whether an amateur has reached this level of sophistication. The amateurs I met were typically modest, even humble, about their attainments. They seemed to sense when they were effectively apprentices, when they had much to learn, and when they needed supervision in excavating a site or more experience before producing a valid set of observations. Even journeymen may feel "inadequate" when comparing themselves with the local professionals with whom they have frequent contact. Like all scientists, journeymen are always learning, expanding their grasp of the discipline as a whole, and absorbing new developments pertinent to their specialties. The same holds for the masters.

The *masters* actually contribute to their science. This they do by collecting original data on their own, data that advance the field. They are aware of certain gaps of knowledge in their specialties. They know how to make the observations that could conceivably close those gaps: they systematically collect the relevant data and publicize them through talks, reports, and journal articles. Any amateur can contribute through serendipity such as the chance discovery of a new celestial object, but masters systematically seek new data through programs they design (e.g., digging their own archaeological sites) or coordinate with others (e.g., working as part of a team spread across the country to observe a lunar occultation.)[3] Master amateur research projects are, however, chiefly exploratory, with theorizing and hypotheses-testing being mostly the domain of the professional (Stebbins 1978a; Weber 1968, 295). If these activities are properly conducted validation of one's status as master follows: amateurs and professionals alike acknowledge the individual's research; journal articles are accepted for publication; and speaking invitations are received.

Two further points remain to be made about this typology. First, the passage of an avocational scientist from apprentice to journeyman is an inexact process. Such development, based on the acquisition of knowledge, experience, and personal confidence, is gradual. Second, it is doubtful that any avocational science society contains a high proportion of masters; 50 percent is probably the upper limit. Although many members are capable of being masters, some find that other leisure interests, not to mention family and work obligations, drain away their time and energy available for steady original research. Furthermore, some amateurs dislike the degree of regimentation and systematization required of a true master. Other activities, such as the fun of looking at the heavens, exploring for minerals, or partaking of the social life of amateurism, hold more appeal. Different types of avocational scientists realize different returns on their entrepreneurial investments.

Pre-Professional Amateurs

The involvements of the pre-professional amateur – the person who is consciously preparing for professional work in his or her pursuit – can also be interpreted as part of the development stage of the amateur-professional career. Preparation may be largely or entirely informal, as it is in the entertainment, sport, and some fine arts areas, or it may be largely formal, as it is in other fine arts and science areas. The difference turns on whether the amateur is chiefly self-taught, although possibly aided by supplementary scraps of advice, informal tutelage, and perhaps a series of lessons or a course or two; or educated in a school, academy, conservatory, or university. Training is informal for pre-professionals in magic, football, writing, pottery, stand-up comedy, and similar fields; it is formal for those in, say, music, ballet, painting, and the sciences.

An array of contingencies and turning points touches one or both categories. This Project, which by and large explored fields where informal preparation is the norm, turned up such contingencies as favouritism, gender discrimination, faulty evaluation by gatekeepers, and "breaks" (both bad and lucky). But because the Project never examined the pre-professionals who go through formal preparation, little will be said here about that process. Federico's (1974, 253–5) study of recruitment and training for a career in ballet suggests that similar contingencies are likely to be encountered there as well.

ESTABLISHMENT

As mentioned, practitioners enter the establishment stage when they feel they have moved beyond the status of learner of the basics. In general, their task is to find a place in the amateur or professional world; in a word, to become established in their pursuit. This process differs for amateurs and professionals, although, to varying degrees, it is stressful for both.

The line between developing as a practitioner and becoming established as such is much hazier for the amateur than the professional. At a point late in development, amateurs begin to routinize the pursuit of their activity in their particular locale. This process involves finding and cultivating opportunities, bearing in mind the individual's leisure time available and their degree of interest in pursuing such opportunities. This highly personal ratio was considered earlier, in more general terms, in the discussion of participants and devotees.

In concrete terms, for most amateurs "getting established" means finding a jazz group that plays, say, three times a month; developing a reputation in local theatre such that one can act in, perhaps, four plays a season; or arranging leisure time so one can excavate a nearby archaeological site, maybe once each weekend. In collectivist undertakings, this quest also hinges on the reputation of the amateur as competent, reliable, and a reasonably likeable person. Without such a reputation, amateurs may find others being hired or invited into a group before themselves. It is during the course of getting known, of developing the desired reputation, that amateurs may face significant stress.

Basically, professionals go through the same process of attempting to enhance their reputation. But the goal, at least at this point in their career, is not so much one of routinizing involvement, but rather of finding work that is more and more agreeable and prestigious. This search may be conducted locally, regionally, nationally, even internationally, depending on how the activity is organized and how willing the professionals are to travel or live away from home. For many, the search begins suddenly, a result of their decision to seek full-time work in the activity. Thus, the line between development and getting established is much sharper for professionals, as compared with most amateurs.

As mentioned in chapter 3, the elite amateurs in sport (e.g., Olympic athletes) have more in common with the professionals in their fields than with their less illustrious non-elite amateur colleagues. Elite amateurs raise to an outstanding level of excellence in the development stage. What they must then do is become established, achieve a high rank on the national team, so they can work toward gold, silver, and bronze medals in the various international competitions. In the present scheme, competing internationally is thought to occur during the maintenance stage of the sports career.

One important factor separating amateurs from professionals entering the career establishment stage is the reaction of the parents to their childrens' choice of lifework. Parents were particularly uneasy about their childrens' decision to seek a career in entertainment and, depending on the field and the sex of offspring, even in art and sport. For example, women starting careers in professional golf and tennis were generally encouraged by their parents (Theberge 1977; Kutner 1983, 250). In contrast, artists of both sexes faced considerable parental opposition when they announced their intention to earn a livelihood from art (Simpson 1981, 54–6). As mentioned earlier, some arts (e.g., ballet, theatre) and many entertainment fields (e.g., magic, comedy) are supposedly home to weird, unsavoury, or deviant people; rife with unmanageable contingencies (including favouritism); and plagued by low or erratic income. This Project revealed that nightclub work is especially scorned for daughters, who are seen as somehow too pure for routine association with the patrons of such places. Also some parents regard sport and entertainment as trivial, a "cute" diversion of amateurs who, with the announcement of professional interests, are seen as having got out of hand. Thus parental resistance becomes another hurdle to be surmounted early in the establishment stage. Often, however, that can only be accomplished by demonstrating how fulfilling and financially rewarding the work can actually be. Many parents do eventually come to accept these occupational decisions, once the possibility of a substantial payoff for their son or daughter is made clear.

The Professional Career

Getting established professionally in the art, science, sport, and entertainment fields is a complex process. Consider the area of fine art. The professional careers of artists are so varied that they defy description, even in a general fashion. The best that can be done, given our present knowledge, is to note some of the differences between individual- and group-based careers in art. In the first category, we find such creative people as writers, painters, sculptors, and jazz singers. To get established, they must acquire a sufficiently good reputation to be considered professional according to the standards used by established professionals in their art world (Truzzi 1978). For the later three, this reputation usually develops first on a local level; that also holds true for writers unless their works are more widely distributed. The establishment stage feeds on success at major turning points; one must, for example, place well in juried exhibitions of the art; gain the favour of such critical mediators as art dealers and chain bookstore owners, who can then bring the participants' works to the public's attention; and receive invitations to contribute to selected displays of the art in question, for example, at art shows, writers' fairs, museum exhibits, and jazz festivals (Gibbons 1979; Rosenblum 1978; Sinha 1979; Basirico 1986; Simpson 1981, ch. 3). Overall, getting established in the individual arts means learning from experience, learning what brings acceptance and rejection from the art world and its public. Getting established also means adding to the foundation of skill and knowledge on which expression of the art rests. The artist knows the basics, having learned them in development, but improvement beyond that base is infinitely possible and a measure of one's standing in the field.

All I have said here about individual artists holds for those in groups as well, except that getting established generally means moving within, or between, collectivities. Symphony musicians, for example, get established by acquiring more responsible and better paid positions within their instrumental section (e.g., moving to principal player) and by moving from less to more prestigious orchestras that also offer longer seasons and better pay (Westby 1960; Faulkner 1973). A similar pattern can be observed in dance (Sutherland 1989, 103–4). In theatre, as the thespian's reputation grows, so too do the number of invitations to try out for lead roles in major productions. Individual jazz musicians may also move from less to more prestigious ensembles or the ensemble may, itself, grow in stature over the years. For a few group-based artists, the process of becoming established may last until they attain the status of soloist or principal and, thus, the opportunity to pursue their art on an individual level.

One common thread running through the establishment stage for many fine artists, whether individual or group-based, is the temptation of commercialism. In part, it may be necessary to "go commercial" simply to make a better living when income from purely artistic work is meagre, a condition created by a combination of low public demand and acute oversupply of the art (Seltzer 1989, 223). Thus, the jazz musician may have to play dance gigs, the singer may have to work in radio commercials, the actor may have to accept parts in dinner theatre, the painter may have to produce water colours for corporate offices (Stebbins 1962; Rosenblum 1978, 32; Federico 1974; Simpson 1981, 58–9; Wilson 1964, 27). At this stage, an unknown, but probably high, proportion of professionals succumb substantially, even entirely, to the attractions of an enhanced standard of living made possible by these outlets for their talents. To the extent that this happens, they leave behind the fine art side of their occupation as well as the public and professional respect accorded to those who shun commercialism.

Another common thread is assessment as a career turning point; witness the audition in the performing arts, the jury assessment in the visual arts, and the evaluation in the literary arts. All artists, both amateur and professional, submit to these assessments at the established stage; many continue to do so well into the maintenance stage and some, particularly writers and actors, continue to the end of their careers. In every instance, the artist provides a sample of his or her work, whether by performing a part, showing paintings or photographs, or submitting a manuscript to a person or committee who then judges its quality. Those who review the sample are true "gatekeepers," in the sense that their judgments lead to acceptance – perhaps an orchestral position, a published short story, or a table at a craft fair – or rejection, with its painful message that the artist must seek success elsewhere.

Discussion of the careers of professional scientists is limited here to those in "institutional" settings: institutes, universities, and research centres. It is their work that is most likely to be published in places where amateurs can read it and subsequently contribute to the same body of knowledge. Scientists who are mission-oriented, who work in government or industry, seldom have amateur counterparts. Both categories, however, have a clear-cut entry into the establishment stage via the research degree, typically a master's or doctoral degree, the "calling card" to professional employment.

Professionals in institutional settings strive to establish their careers by cultivating reputations as worthy contributors to one or several specialties within a discipline. Presentations of their research at major conferences and its subsequent publication in respectable journals or in books published by reputable houses are the main ways to accomplish this. Promotion to the rank of associate professor (in North America) is also a reasonably valid indicator of passage from the establishment to the maintenance stage. Such promotion usually means that the scientist has developed a research program of some value to his or her discipline, contributed to it sufficiently by means of publications, and is therefore viewed as willing and able to continue this routine for many years. It goes without saying that this is a time of considerable insecurity.

Receiving research grants and fellowships, awards for research excellence, and prestigious speaking engagements are among the ways that establishment is nurtured in institutionally based science. In addition, a high rate of output of publications of acceptable quality will accelerate progress to the next career stage. Excellence in such activities as teaching (in universities) and administration are two other ways of measuring merit, although they are usually seen as less important than the ability to contribute directly to the growth of the science. Mahoney's (1976, ch. 4 and 5) review of the scientific career indicates that here, too, there are gatekeepers, such as editors, referees, deans, and department heads, who affect the practitioner's career progress.

In sport, the establishment stage begins when a player is hired by a professional team or placed on the professional list in an individual sport. This is a major turning point, although in team sport it is contingent on such chance factors as the quality of competitors for the position and the availability of positions. For similar reasons, getting drafted to a team and being allowed to attend its training camp (in team sport) is, technically speaking, a pre-establishment, contingent turning point.

Whereas professional athletes must always compete for their place on the professional list or team, data from this Project suggest that they typically reach a point at which this competition becomes more or less routine. In team sport, for example, they work their way up to a starting position, where they can feel reasonably secure that more junior players will not outdo them. This is the point at which the sports professional passes from the establishment to the maintenance phase.

As in the other areas, awards can speed progress through the establishment stage. I found players in team sports to be especially concerned about their "stats," the set of quantitative measures for their performance (e.g., batting averages, number of pass receptions, average points per game). The better the stats, the better the chances of winning a starting position on the team. Finally, those players who become popular with the fans are helping to establish themselves, to the extent that they are seen as an asset in ticket sales.

Professional establishment in the individual sports means reaching a consistent level of winnings from meets, matches, and tournaments, such that they sufficiently offset the costs of participation and leave enough on which to live. Such a level is only possible if the player continues to improve beyond the development stage, for winnings are directly related to level of placement in each tournament. Theberge (1980), Kutner (1983, 252–4), and Allison and Meyer (1988) all report that, for women's professional golf and tennis, this is a highly stressful stage of one's career.

The gatekeeping function, as fulfilled by tryouts in the fine arts, is also evident in team sport. During training camp and, later, during the season, coaches and personnel managers evaluate the competence of recruits as well as regular players. In individual sport, however, gatekeepers do not exist at the establishment stage, since players advance on the basis of points earned for participating and placing in different tournaments stratified by level of prestige.

Passage into the establishment stage in entertainment is typically gradual, unless the performer is hired and paid a steady wage by an organization such as a circus or chain of comedy clubs. Like the individual fine artist, the freelancing entertainer must try to improve his or her act and build a reputation that makes possible a steady living from the art. This calls for, among other approaches, self-promotion with flyers and posted notices, showcasing at various nightclubs, and advertising in the appropriate mass media. Some entertainers sign with a booking agent; some hire a personal manager whose job is to help them improve and find work. In all this, each hopes to advance to increasingly better paying engagements, performed in increasingly prestigious and appealing locations. It often means quitting the road and finding steady work in and around a major urban centre.

To succeed, artists must seek all possible experience. If remunerative work is insufficient, they sometimes resort to "busking," or street entertainment, a common alternative. Friedman (1990) learned that aspiring Hollywood actors in this situation often seek work in television commercials as a stopgap. Indeed, with a hat, box, or musical instrument case open to passerby, many a juggler, magician, musician, pantomime, and stunt artist has supplemented income earned from more formal gigs. Formal gigs and busking sessions provide experience and ideas for polishing an act or turning it into consistently good entertainment. It is in connection with formal gigs that entertainers encounter their species of gatekeeper: the booking agent, nightclub manager, festival organizer, and the like.

In sum, the establishment stage of the professional career in art, science, sport, and entertainment is probably the most stressful of all. For one, the practitioners at this point are especially vulnerable; newcomers with high aspirations, they are naïve to a significant degree regarding the workings of the professional world. We shall see in the next chapter that they are also often subject to exploitation, favouritism, and capricious or poorly informed judgments concerning their ability and potential (from critics, reviewers, coaches, directors, etc.). Often, too, financial insecurity is high during this period, linked as it is to intense competition for a limited number of opportunities. Jealousy and backbiting, although problems for professionals throughout their career, are perhaps most unsettling during this establishment stage. It is no wonder that a significant, yet still unknown, proportion of practitioners abandon altogether their push to get established, either returning to amateur status or leaving the activity altogether. Clearly, if professionals are to survive to the next career stage, they must successfully navigate two important turning points: the acquisition of sufficient ability, and the marshalling of sufficient dedication.

MAINTENANCE

During the maintenance stage, the amateur-professional career is in full bloom, in the sense that practitioners are now able to enjoy the pursuit to its utmost. In entertainment, they are typically a headliner; in academic science, at least an associate professor; in sport, a household name; and, in art, a recognized and respected professional in local, regional, or national art circles. Maintenance ends with decline, retirement, career change, or death. It is the period during which the practitioner experiences the maximum number of rewards and the minimum number of costs, a time when life is "good," at least when compared with what went before. Nonetheless, life during maintenance is never an unalloyed joy. Professional and amateur careers are rarely that at any stage.

Competition, for example, is always there. The practitioner is only better prepared now to meet it. Nor do jealousy, favouritism, backbiting, and capricious judgments go away. Indeed, they may actually increase. At the lofty height of maintenance, artists, scientists, and so on have simply learned to cope with these human foibles. They do, however, know the ropes better than ever: how to avoid exploitation, prevent trouble, handle competitors, find the best work, and the like. Nonetheless, when exploitation is built into the activity itself, as in professional sport (Beamish 1982; Garvey 1979, 92), escape is only partial.

Having reached the maintenance stage in no way suggests that all mountains have now been climbed. Indeed, early maintenance may be a time for professionals to map out strategies for scaling new peaks, some of which may never be conquered. Many a classical music soloist, for instance, hopes to appear in Carnegie Hall. Only a few ever do so. Every professional athlete wants to be on a team that wins the World Series, the Stanley Cup, the Super Bowl, or the World Cup. Many retire disappointed. This Project demonstrated that maintenance, too, has its stresses, disappointments, and disillusionments. Faulkner (1975, 537) notes that part of the subjective career at this stage is coming to grips with these realities and with one's probable level of success.

In certain fields, the two major contingencies are injury and sickness. Athletes, dancers, acrobats, and others whose careers are limited by declining physical capacity can be even further hindered by injury or extended sickness. Such possibilities hang like the sword of Damocles over the heads of practitioners. In fact, an injury may not only remove players or artists from active participation for long periods of time, but can leave them in less than complete recovery – with a permanent condition that restricts physical mobility long after the period of inactivity has come to an end.

Because many practitioners spend more time in maintenance than in any other stage of their career, they face a number of special structural and cultural contingencies. For instance, changes abound in taxation policies, arts funding, audience tastes, team ownership, availability of research funds, television programming, and so on. As a result some professionals may be fired; others will find less work than previously. To the extent that they rely on private or public sector funding, amateur pursuits are affected as well. Security at this stage is sometimes only relatively better than during the establishment period.

As noted, the maintenance stage can end in one of four ways: death, retirement, career change, or decline. Death is self-explanatory. Retirement refers to leaving the work force altogether. Changing careers means entering a new line of work or leisure, a line that may or may not be related to the abandoned line. Thus, the academic scientist might become a dean, the baseball player a coach, the symphony violinist a conservatory professor, the stand-up comic a film actor. Here, too, one's sex may be a contingency. For example, Hanna (1988, 121) reports that ballerinas are conspicuously under-represented in such non-dancing second careers as choreographer-composer and director-manager. Although pursuit of the earlier professional activity may continue on a post-professional amateur or a part-time professional basis (with remuneration), the principal occupation, however pursued, is now different. A career change is the usual response for practitioners who face decline before occupational retirement is reached.

DECLINE

Decline is most threatening in the highly physical amateur-professional pursuits where, as one anonymous wag put it, "the road to ruin is always in good repair." We mentioned that injury can sometimes set premature decline in motion. Aging, however, is probably the number one enemy and main contingency here; its effects are felt earliest in the most strenuous activities, among them dance, football, hockey, boxing, basketball, and soccer. Decline comes later in fields such as orchestral music, where players in their fifties may find themselves being moved further back in the section as the years go by (Westby 1960). With aging comes waning physical power, a slow and imperceptible process. It quietly contradicts the myth that, whether we work in sport, dance, or some other field, we have drunk from the fountain of youth and therefore have no need to worry about physical decline, especially at so young an age as thirty.

At this stage of the sports career, some players confront a second contingency: the availability of lower level, professional playing opportunities as in, for example, the minor leagues in baseball and hockey and the satellite tours in tennis and golf (Ball 1976). Unfortunately for the Canadian football player, there are only a few scattered senior teams in existence. The hapless, aging player is simply put out to pasture – relegated to the general labour market – and replaced by a younger player with a brighter and longer athletic future.

Decline and retirement in sport are somewhat easier to accept when the alternatives are appealing, when the player has prepared for an interesting second, or non-playing, career inside or outside the game. But what second career can match the glamour, salary, and excitement of professional sport? I find that level of education is a contingency here, for it is usually only in jobs requiring a university or professional degree that an ex-athlete can even begin to approach these kinds of rewards. In this regard, an outstanding reputation in a professional sport may help its retirees find, although not necessarily keep, a better than average non-playing job (Hearle, Jr., 1975, 507). Nevertheless, the broad picture is one of many former professionals working at blue-collar jobs at a young age, with young families to support (in soccer, see Houlston 1982). So acute is this problem in dance that Canada opened the Dancer Transition Centre in 1985.

According to evidence at hand, the retirement comedown is likely to be severe only in high-level professional sport (Coakley 1987; Greendorfer and Blinde 1987). Studies of males retiring from university football and basketball (Kleiber, Greendorfer et al., 1987; Adler and Adler 1991, 218) and Canadian junior hockey (Curtis and Ennis 1988) suggest that life satisfaction can be considerable after retirement, especially if the player leaves the sport on a positive note (with an award, a good playing season, or a team championship). Satisfaction was measured by attitudes toward life in general, post-retirement employment, and marital status. A study of retired Polish Olympians found that they had retained high social status and a significant role in social and cultural life (Pawluk 1984). And Allison and Meyer's (1988) study of female tennis professionals revealed a strong sense of relief upon retirement, coupled with a desire to resume a normal life-style.

A much more nebulous contingency at this stage is *creative decline,* a problem that chiefly afflicts artists and entertainers. This condition may result from occupational burnout, which in stand-up comedy can result from too many jobs on the road during which the comic, instead of "killing" the audience with laughter, performs on "automatic pilot." In artistic burnout, expression of the art becomes routine, humdrum; it is dull for both the public and the artist. Soon a public response to the stagnation occurs and opportunities to produce or display one's art diminish sharply. To reverse this trend, the practitioner must somehow find inspiration, whether by developing new material (entertainment), playing new works (music), or acting in a different genre of drama (theatre).

Moreover, entertainment and even fine art can be somewhat faddish, in that certain styles may come and go with alarming rapidity. Adler (1975, 364) observed that, for today's painters, "the period between the initiation of innovating or even deliberately provocative works and their final appearance and eventual eulogy by formerly conservative cultural institutions such as museums and established critics has radically contracted." This is because vanguard artists are now the elite of today's art world, which means that fashionable art becomes "obsolete" (loses its public appeal) as soon as another innovation hits the market. This set of circumstances signals the beginning of career decline, unless the artist can rebound with still another exciting innovation. As Simpson (1981, 76) observes, in the art world "originality, more than the mastery of craftsmanship, is the key to success."

But one substantial attraction of many amateur-professional pursuits, especially those outside sport, is that practitioners can often elude decline and even forced retirement. They persist into ripe old age as full-time professionals, among them, Pablo Casals, Vladimir Horowitz, Albert Einstein, George Burns, Bob Hope, and Ernest Hemingway. Many a local amateur has followed the same path. Alternatively, the practitioner may reduce involvement to some degree, moving to part-time professional status where he or she can continue to make money, or to post-professional amateur status where participation is now purely for the enjoyment of it all. All in all, there are a number of routes to follow should the practitioner move beyond the career stage of maintenance.

CHAPTER SIX

Costs and Rewards

The etymological root of the word "amateur" is the Latin *amator*, or one who loves. In our case, it is one who loves one's avocation. Common sense has it that that love is the singular, indeed fundamental, motive for pursuing any amateur activity. How convenient it would be if amateurism were so easily explained. Unfortunately, however, it is not. What is worse, the common sense explanation, while true as far as it goes, neglects two incontrovertible facts. First, although it is possible that amateurs are more attracted to their pursuits than their professional colleagues, perhaps because they participate in them less, these activities are nonetheless seldom pure bliss for either category. Amateurs, as already noted, do get tired, bored, frustrated, peeved, and discouraged just as professionals do; the acquisition, maintenance, and expression of skill and knowledge always entail some negative aspects.

Second, professionals love their work, too. Yet, the common sense explanation implies that they dislike it, apparently because they *have* to do it to live. This stance fails to square with the sixth ideal-typical attribute of these usually dedicated practitioners; namely, that they tend to place standards and service ahead of material rewards. In addition, as mentioned, both professionals and amateurs often find the competition in their fields attractive. In reality, much of professional work is so engaging that it becomes an end in itself, erasing the lines between work and leisure (Pavalko 1988, 179; Orzack 1959).

That there are rewards *and* costs in amateurism suggests the profit hypothesis from the exchange framework as a more effective explanation of the leisure motives of amateurs than the one based on common sense: "The greater the profit [excess of reward over cost] a person receives as a result of his action, the more likely he is to perform the action" (Homans 1974, 31).

This proposition can organize research data on the motives of amateurs in a way consistent with the amateurs' similarity to, and close ties with, the professionals in their field. Hence the aim of this chapter is to demonstrate that those who pursue an avocation *do* experience a profit. The chapter's principal thesis is that, although occasional costs may be endured by these amateurs in the conduct of their pastime, in the end, these costs are substantially offset by the rewards found therein. We shall see that the same may be said for their professional counterparts. The chief advantage of Homans's hypothesis, compared with the common sense assumption, is that Homans recognizes the seemingly inescapable negative element present in human activities. Applied to leisure, this theory suggests that, even in this sphere of our lives, there may be odious accompaniments. These, moreover, are especially likely to be present when leisure is taken seriously, as amateurism is. It takes a noticeable profit to keep us voluntarily at such activities.

The main part of this chapter is devoted to a description of the comparative costs and rewards in the art, science, sport, and entertainment worlds. It should be understood that no test of Homans's hypothesis is intended here. Rather it is used strictly as an *ad hoc* explanation and an organizational principle. We must still adopt a measure of profit, however, that is independent of the definition of this concept (excess of reward over cost). Such a measure is discussed in the concluding section. It should also be noted that the data on costs and rewards were gathered apropos amateurs in seven of the eight fields (excluding music) and apropos professionals in magic, football, and stand-up comedy.

REWARDS

The rewards of a pursuit, those more or less routine values that attract and hold its practitioners, must be distinguished from the accompanying thrills (these latter will be covered in the next section). During the research on amateurs and professionals, a list of nine rewards eventually emerged, rewards that were found to attract practitioners to their vocations or avocations.[1] All nine were found in every field studied, although each was ranked in a different order of importance. As the following list shows, the rewards of amateur-professional pursuits are mostly personal:

Personal rewards
• Self-actualization
• Self-expression
• Self-conception

- Self-gratification
- Self-enrichment
- Re-creation (regeneration)
- Monetary returns

Social rewards
- Social attraction
- Group accomplishment

Self-actualization, or *self-realization*, refers to the opportunity offered participants via the amateur activity to develop their talents, skills, or knowledge; to fulfill part of their potential as human beings. The expression of these talents, skills, and knowledge, to the extent that they have already been developed, is an additional reward. Enhanced *self-conception* results from the favourable social identity associated with a particular field. *Self-gratification* is the label given the aspect of pure enjoyment linked to an amateur-professional pursuit.[2] It is the only reward in the list that is essentially hedonistic. The unusual, memorable experiences found in the activity contribute to *self-enrichment* by endowing the individual with moral, cultural, or intellectual resources. *Re-creation*, or *regeneration*, is a strictly amateur reward; it refers to the capacity of the activity to divert the practitioner's mind from work or from the other events and problems in life that absorb attention. For professionals, and even some amateurs, a pursuit can also be *financially rewarding*.

The two social rewards, social attraction and group accomplishments, share the component of "fun," the feeling of participating with others in an attractive activity (Podilchak 1988). The first reward – social attraction – denotes the camaraderie that develops around a pursuit, the appeal of talking about it, and the exhilaration of being part of the scene. The second reward – group accomplishment, possible only in collective undertakings such as team sports and the concerted arts – is the reward that comes from having done one's part in a collaborative project.

This list elaborates and extends Dumazedier's (1967, 14–17) three functions of leisure: relaxation, entertainment, and personal development. His relaxation corresponds to our re-creation, in that it promotes recovery from fatigue, boredom, and tension. Entertainment, since it refers to the satisfying side of leisure, corresponds to our self-gratification. The remaining personal reasons listed above are forms of Dumazedier's personal development. The social reasons appear to have no parallel in his classification and so constitute an extension of it.

The foregoing list of rewards gives substance to the observation made in chapter 1 that amateurs, and for that matter professionals, pursue their vocations and avocations primarily for self-interested reasons. From the perspective of the sociology of knowledge, the self-interestedness of modern amateurs and professionals bears a strong resemblance to the economic individualism of the capitalist societies in which they thrive. The earlier depiction of amateurs and professionals as entrepreneurs is also in line with this observation. Of the four elements of economic individualism – competitiveness, possessiveness, achievement, and personal welfare – only the first was not uniformly observed throughout this Project. The amateur scientists were less competitive than their counterparts in art, sport, and entertainment, areas where judgments of excellence play a central role in the activity.

With this background, let us now turn to the main patterns of rewards that emerged in the fields studied.

Patterns of Rewards

Self-enrichment constituted the most powerful and widespread reward in all the fields studied, both amateur and professional. In the theatre arts, it was evident in the rapport that often develops between audience and performer: the delicate emotional communications through which the actor makes the audience laugh, cry, wonder, admire, and the like (see also Kohansky 1984, 4–5). This communicative process is called the "gift of laughter" in comedy. Self-enrichment also refers to singular experiences, such as those found in sport, science, and theatre: the exhilaration of competition (in baseball, see Hearle, Jr. 1975, 482), the thrill of gazing into space through a high-powered telescope, the enriching experience of portraying a person vastly different from oneself, the vicarious thrill of living in the archaeological past. In addition, being onstage is a source of enrichment – dubbed the "limelighter role" in magic – whether as a single entertainer, soloist in music, principal in theatre, or batter or pitcher in baseball. Nowhere is serious leisure so clearly set apart from casual leisure as in these moments; they offer a reward that can only be realized from a base of developed knowledge and skill and expressed at special points in time, in special places.

Self-gratification – the reward that also forms the basis for casual leisure – ran a close second to self-enrichment in terms of importance to both amateurs and professionals. Self-gratification was, however, more rewarding for those in sport and entertainment than for those in art and science. We would expect sports such as baseball and football to be enjoyable, whether played at an amateur or a professional level. Although enjoyableness is an inherent quality of sports and games, the connection between gratification and performing as an entertainer is less obvious. It seems to be the levity of entertainment – its hallmark – that encourages both performers and consumers to describe it as hedonistically enjoyable. Entertainment is, and is supposed to be, lighthearted, conducted in an atmosphere of pure gratification.

In the domains of art, sport, and science, where a clear set of skills or body of knowledge, or both, form the foundation of each pursuit, self-actualization and self-expression tended to be valued as highly as that of self-gratification. Moreover, of the first two, self-expression was generally given somewhat more weight (by artists and scientists). Magicians and baseball players said self-expression was a major reward. It was also a main reward in theatre, where to interpret and present a role creatively is an honoured ability that takes years to develop. In astronomy, knowledge of one's chosen speciality is the first requirement; among amateurs, however, that is only useful if it is backed up with knowledge of how to "get around the sky" with a field telescope. David Sudnow (1978, xii–xiii) discusses the reward of self-actualization and self-expression in the following introspective account of how he became a jazz piano player:

From an upright position I look down and see my fingers, and my looking is so differently related to the work of the fingers, in contrast to former modes of "hookup," that I see things I never saw before, because these happenings never occurred before. I see my hands for the first time now as "jazz piano player's hands," and at times, when I expressly think about it, one sense I have from my vantage point looking down is that the fingers are making the music all by themselves. As I watch the letters coming up on the page when typing rapidly along, thinking the thought as my typing, as I watch the thought seeming to settle down on the page as the competent flycaster smoothly sets a lure gently down on a trout pond, I wonder, had I a similar historical access to the looks of my fingers at this typewriter keyboard, would I see "fingers doing thinking"?

My hands have come to develop an intimate knowledge of the piano keyboard, ways of exploratory engagement with routings through its spaces, modalities of reaching and articulating, and now I choose places to go in the course of moving from place to place as a handful choosing.

A combination of self-expression and self-actualization has also been characterized as a main reward among racquetball players and female golfers (Theberge 1980; Spreitzer and Snyder 1983).

But from here on, the pattern of rewards for the various fields became much more idiosyncratic. Self-conception generally ranked next, thus constituting a secondary reward in art, sport, and entertainment.

It was scarcely mentioned, however, in amateur science, although recognition as a valued contributor to a body of knowledge is greatly sought after among professionals (Mahoney 1976, 119). After self-conception came the social rewards. Group accomplishment was placed at about the same level in sport and the collective arts (i.e., theatre, baseball, and football). Social attraction as a reward was even less important, with the exceptions of archaeology and baseball. Procedure in amateur archaeology may help explain the social appeal of the science: practitioners usually work together when excavating or surveying a site. Regeneration after work was the second most important reward in theatre, but was either never mentioned or accorded only a low rank in the remaining fields. Finally, monetary return was ranked third by professionals in magic and football and sixth by those in stand-up comedy and female golf (Theberge 1980).[3] It is a minor or nonexistent reward for all amateurs, even for those in magic, who are expected to charge a fee for their shows.

Thrills

Thrills, the sharply exciting events and occasions that stand out in the minds of amateurs and professionals, are extraordinary rewards. In all eight studies, they were often but not uniformly associated with the rewards of self-enrichment and, to a lesser extent, self-actualization and self-expression. That is, the thrills in the four amateur-professional areas may be seen as manifestations of more abstract rewards; they are what the practitioners in each field seek as concrete expressions of the rewards found therein.

In the realm of serious leisure and professional work, the thrills are many and varied. In the arts, they constitute the great moments onstage when rapport with the audience is at its peak and performers are at their best. As for science, it is thrilling to discover something such as a comet or burial site. Avocational astronomers said it was particularly thrilling to observe known processes and phenomena under optimal conditions. In the words of an amateur:

There are times like, for example, when you're observing a planet just like Jupiter and if you've got a good instrument and the ceiling settles right down, you can see with your naked eye (through a scope) more than has even been photographed with the biggest telescope anywhere. Like I've seen detail on Jupiter that has only been seen in a photograph when they've sent satellites there. This stuff is just a fleeting instance. You've got maybe a second when just all of a sudden everything is just working right. The detail is just inspiring ... Your instrument itself, it works more or less well depending on how much the temperature is changing and stuff like that. So, when the conditions get right, there are times when that can be very inspiring.

One of the main thrills in sport comes from playing in championship games, a sentiment that is clearly underscored when one's team wins. For many amateurs, simply playing exceptionally well in a regular game is thrilling. In entertainment, as in the performing fine arts, just to be onstage in an atmosphere of high audience rapport can also be thrilling. It is on these occasions in stand-up comedy that the comic "kills."

Thrills are also found in significant career advances. They come from being signed (for the first time) by a professional team, opening a show featuring a star comic, publishing one's first scientific article, or landing a "plum" role in a major play. Some respondents, chiefly young adult amateurs, said it was thrilling to meet a famous practitioner in their field. Among professional magicians, it was a rare career thrill to be invited to perform at the Magic Castle in Los Angeles, the private clubhouse of the Academy of Magical Arts.

THE BENEFITS OF WORK AND LEISURE

The Project demonstrates that the thrills and rewards of amateur-professional pursuits are considerable; that together they constitute a powerful motivational foundation for these types of work and leisure. Scattered evidence from studies of other amateur-professional pursuits in art and sport lends further support to this conclusion. Musicians and dancers, for instance, have been shown to experience audience-performer rapport just as self-enriching as that of actors (see Finnegan 1989, 158–9; Hanna 1988, 121). Self-enrichment in the individual arts is a different, but clearly major, reward, at least for painters.

The most frequently mentioned reason for painting can be categorized as entailing some form of "discovery" or "understanding ..." One of the main rewards artists obtain from their work is a stronger grasp on the world that surrounds them. This is not an intellectual knowledge in the usual sense but an existential, intuitive, visual understanding of themselves in relation to other people and objects. The discovery of how they relate to the rest of the world through the process of artistic creation is an important source of satisfaction for young artists. (Getzels and Csikszentmihalyi 1976, 20)

Many female golf and tennis professionals say that successful competition is a strong and personally enriching reward (Kutner 1983, 258;

Theberge 1980; Allison and Meyer 1988). Dance, with its body movement, can engender pure enjoyment (self-gratification) (Hanna 1988, 120), as can manipulation of words in poetry (Wilson 1964, 7). In these fields, as in those considered in this Project, financial rewards are important to professionals. Yet money is usually accorded a lower rank than the aforementioned intrinsic rewards, since the low income so common in art and sport forces the practitioner to seek satisfaction elsewhere.

One question that I pondered as I developed the present, grounded theoretic elaboration of my earlier studies focused on the nature of the gender differences in the various patterns of rewards and thrills found in amateur-professional activities. Neither the studies cited in the preceding paragraph nor those I conducted suggested any differences whatsoever. To be sure, some studies were conducted on homogeneous samples of men or women, whereas others involved small samples of women and large samples of men. Nevertheless, I suspect that differences exist, and that, to uncover them, more careful phenomenological work than has been undertaken so far will be necessary. For instance, men and women may both regard athletic competition as enriching, but in more or less different ways or for more or less different reasons. At any rate, the dearth of information on gender differences here may be due more to a failure to ask the right questions than to a true absence of such differences.

DISAPPOINTMENTS

We turn now to the costs of serious leisure and professional work, one category of which is the disappointments found there. Disappointments can be defined as the absence of expected rewards and their manifestations. Thus they are born in the failure of high hopes. In fact, because the disappointments tended to be specific to each area, it was impossible to develop a list of generalized disappointments, as I did for the rewards.[4] Indeed, the only generalization applicable to all areas would be that many professionals and somewhat fewer amateurs develop, as a result of experience, a cautious attitude toward their pursuits. They learn to avoid high hopes that can founder on the rocks of failure. But even here there is variation from area to area.

In sport, for example, it is thrilling to play in a championship game and bitterly disappointing to lose. Both amateurs and professionals hold this sentiment, for both categories of player hope to win during the game. As disappointing, although for somewhat fewer players, is being sidelined by injury or illness, especially for a major part of the season. More or less third in prevalence is the individual's disappointment that stems from a poor performance in a particular game (in golf and tennis see Theberge 1980, 34; Allison and Meyer 1988), or a poor performance by the team throughout the season. In all instances, there were no differences here between amateurs and professionals. This is as it should be, inasmuch as all athletes are trained to think positively about the outcome of each contest in which they participate, to believe that they can win if they give their best.[5]

At the opposite extreme, we find a relative absence of disappointment in amateur science. A substantial majority of respondents in archaeology and astronomy, for example, said that they avoided disappointments by avoiding high hopes. Working as they did in the exploratory end of their sciences (Stebbins 1978a), they had faint hope of finding something whose nature had yet to be discovered (e.g., an Indian burial site, the brightness of a variable star). Amateurs in astronomy were careful to point out that, although frequently frustrated by weather conditions, they only allowed themselves to become disappointed when rare celestial phenomena or processes, such as a solar eclipse or a famous comet, were obscured by fog or clouds. Mahoney (1976, 113) reports that the routine nature of much of normal (confirmatory) science engenders a noticeable level of frustration and disappointment among professional scientists.

The most frequent disappointment in theatre stemmed from the actors' inability to perfect a major part to their taste. Indeed, it is simply impossible, at times, to identify with a character. Perhaps the actors simply lacked the time required to achieve an acceptable interpretation, a problem that can also plague amateur classical musicians who are in the course of preparing a concerto or lengthy orchestral solo. As for failing an audition, it is disappointing in every performing art.

While bombing in comedy was a relatively common disappointment for amateurs and even some professionals (everybody bombs once in a while), the equivalent in magic – lack of the expected audience response to a trick – was a source of disappointment for less than a quarter of the sample. This discrepancy can be explained, in part, by the different audience reactions to magic tricks and comic monologues. Mind you, the absence of wonderment after a trick intended to amaze is more difficult to discern than the absence of laughter following a line intended to amuse. As the comics put it, the silence is "deafening" at this point. Consistent with this observation is the finding that, in general, the amateur and professional magicians were more likely to be free of disappointments (and high hopes) than the comics. Still, a number of magicians were occasionally disappointed when a trick "flopped" or failed to materialize as planned. In addition, comics, whose work opportunities are controlled significantly by such intermediaries as nightclub managers and booking agents, sometimes cited slow career advancement as a disappointment.

DISLIKES

When I asked my interviewees to identify and discuss their dislikes apropos their pursuits, I indicated that I was interested in more serious matters than simply pet peeves. Dislikes, I said, are problems that require the practitioner to adjust significantly, possibly even to leave the pursuit. As with disappointments, the dislikes tended to pertain to a specific field or area. The only possible generalization applicable to all four areas was that professionals have more dislikes than do amateurs, a finding that squares with the greater continuance commitment of the former (see chapter 3).

Of all the fields studied, astronomy had the lowest proportion of amateurs with dislikes (50 percent). The most prevalent of these dislikes was the active data collection by some amateur members of the local clubs. These were the "armchair astronomers," who preferred to read about, and listen to lectures on, their science. The two other dislikes – for cliques and for poorly organized club events – were mentioned much less frequently.

The disparagement of amateurs by certain professionals was the only identified widespread dislike in amateur archaeology (held by approximately 40 percent of the sample) (see also Turnbaugh 1983). The view that amateurs conduct inferior science was an evaluation I heard (or sensed) while in the company of professionals. In fact, some professional astronomers hold similar views (Lankford 1979; Rothenberg 1981; Williams 1983), but these views rarely reach the ears of amateurs. No doubt that attitude reflects the lack of opportunities for interaction. For example, whereas amateur and professional archaeologists often work together on excavations, in astronomy, the two types of scientists work separately most of the time.

In theatre, it was the poorly motivated actor who topped the list of dislikes, a type who is also well known in music and sport. These are fields where a systematic effort to learn the art or sport is expected of all participants. But some (marginal) amateurs want to participate without going through the "drudgery" of preparation (conditioning, learning, practising, and so on; in music, see Roberts 1991a, 118–21). Their inadequate preparation not only drags down the overall quality of the group's performance, but also spoils the fun of the serious leisure participants, who are then forced to perform with inferior amateurs.

A smaller number of actors lamented the presence of incompetent directors. Such people can waste time at rehearsals, handle amateurs ineptly, and know too little about the play itself or the art of acting and staging (at times a combination of all three) (see also Lyon 1982). A third significant dislike was the "know-it-all" of theatre, the person who thinks he or she is wiser about the art and piece being rehearsed than the director. In the face of incompetent directors, this stance is possible defensible; certainly not otherwise. Only two respondents in the theatre sample had no dislikes at all.

Favouritism is a hot issue in certain amateur-professional fields, although not in others. Whereas audition committees now help control it in the fine arts area (e.g., Hinton-Braaten 1980), in the domain of sport, given the absence of an equivalent structure, it constitutes the number one dislike. There both amateurs and professionals complained about it. In professional football, charges of favouritism were mingled with accusations of unfairness, dishonesty, and inconsistency in the way management deals with players. This in practical terms, is the "politics" of sport.

Another poignant dislike in sport, chiefly found among amateur baseball and junior football players, is the undermotivated teammate. University and professional football are too competitive for any extensive development of this dislike; indeed, such players are soon cut or benched, replaced with more enthusiastic team members. At the lower end of adult amateur sport, we found a dislike of the incompetent coach, with his weak communication with players, ineffective game strategies, and poorly developed knowledge of technique – a phenomenon similar to that observed in theatre. Finally, all amateurs lamented – some stating it as a dislike – the slight to non-existent coverage of their team's activities by the local mass media. Many felt that high school sport received more attention.

Canadian professional football players had their own list of dislikes, some or all of which could be valid for other professional sports inside and outside Canada. Most upsetting was the widespread practice of using the team trainer to authenticate as minor an injury that was actually, or potentially, incapacitating if subjected to further play. The powerful desire to win the next game drives a number of coaches and managers to pressure their trainers into lying to players in this way. Nearly as hated is the tendency among some reporters from the "written" press to distort the comments players make in interviews in order to support the reporter's analysis of what happened inside the team or on the playing field. Indeed, the players held that the typical sports reporter, sitting in the press box, knows little about the actual game being played on the field.

Magicians at both levels listed their principal dislike as the weak acts that reflect unfavourably on magic as a genre of entertainment. Comics chafed at their public image as happy-go-lucky people leading a profligate life of sex and drugs during the pursuit of a marginal night-time occupation that pokes fun at society. Both sets of artists shared a hearty distaste for bad audiences in general and, particularly, for members who heckle, steal material, drink too much, or gather in boisterous clusters. They considered "stealing" material, which refers to the theft of tricks, patter, humorous lines, and other original components of a performer's act, to be an offense. As well, both types of entertainers detested the all too frequent requirement that they perform in seriously inadequate circumstances, exemplified by insufficient lighting, excessive background noise, competing attractions (e.g., darts matches, televised hockey games), inferior sound systems, and cramped or non-existent stages. Both magicians and stand-up comics also commented on the disagreeable personalities of certain colleagues: their vanity, arrogance, ingratiation, or maliciousness; some are reputed backbiters or chronic complainers. As for professionals, they are averse to amateurs who force their entertainment wares on them, more or less demanding that they observe the performance of a trick or monologue and comment favourably upon its completion. Mind you, amateur comics and magicians, along with their counterparts in archaeology, dislike the disparaging remarks of professionals, although the practice just mentioned suggests that, in this regard, these amateurs may be bringing on some of their own trouble.

The comics, because of their closer ties with booking agents and nightclub managers, had certain dislikes not shared by the magicians. For example, the professional comics intensely disliked the "bad agent," or the person who fails to promote them, who promises fees and working conditions that never materialize, or negotiates a low fee with a club manager for their services. "Bad club managers" commit similar sins. In addition to failing to deal decisively with hecklers, they are known to offer seamy lodging or require that the comics collect tickets to their own performances. As in football, so in comedy: again, one must contend with politics, centred, as noted before, on favouritism. Female comics, for example, feel that they are less often favoured by agents and club managers than their male counterparts, and several amateurs believe that certain of their number have "an inside track" with the manager. Finally, amateurs and professionals, alike, disliked being trapped in a contract with a manager or an agent whose judgment and fairness they suspected.

TENSIONS

The tensions found in the amateur-professional pursuits are the most general of the associated costs. We have already discussed, in chapter 3, one major tension that touches every field in which some sort of public performance occurs; namely, stage fright. It is wide-spread throughout sport, entertainment, and the performing arts. It is even present in science when scientists present their work publicly, although, as mentioned earlier, science had by far the lowest proportion of respondents reporting tensions of any sort.

The only other tension in science – interpersonal friction – was mentioned infrequently in my studies. Here I refer to negative, unpleasant relationships rather than types of disagreeable personalities (one of the dislikes examined earlier). In fact, interpersonal friction is possible throughout the amateur-professional world. Occasionally, a practitioner does come to envy, despise, disrespect, or in some way regard with jaundice, a colleague – whether peer, agent, coach, manager, or professional (or amateur). Yet many professionals and amateurs are free of interpersonal friction, and many others experience it with reference to only one or two people.

The try-outs and auditions in the areas of art, sport, and entertainment are stressful for many of the participants. Where the aspirants are confident and the competition is at or below their level of ability, however, there may actually be more eager anticipation than tension. Indeed, approximately 20 percent of the amateur theatre sample indicated that they actually enjoy try-outs. They felt auditions offer the opportunity to parade their excellence and land the part or position along the way. Among the causes of tension, for those who experience it, are stage fright, incompetent gatekeepers, patronage as found in old boy networks, and discrimination along the lines of sex, style, and ethnicity (see, for example, Hinton-Braaten 1980; Merrill 1970, 252; Lyon 1974, 82; Roberts 1991a, 148–60). Amateurs and junior professionals are more likely than others in their fields to be tense.

The audition is not without its equivalent in the individual fine arts. Painters, sculptors, photographers, and craft workers must face a set of intermediaries whose judgments deny or allow access to certain shows, galleries, and museums. Career advancement hangs in the balance. Until artists are well established, rejection will always lurk in the shadows, a stark reminder that their work may be unappreciated in some significant way by those who count. Poets and novelists endure similar evaluations at the hands of editors. It is possible that amateurs and junior professionals experience more tension during such sessions than do senior professionals, since the latter are likely to have had their work evaluated more often and have, thereby, become somewhat hardened to rejection.

In sport, referees' calls are a common source of momentary but, if seen as crucial, lingering tension. Even though players are well aware that the outcome of a game depends on all the plays made during it by both teams, they are still likely to get angry over what seems to them bad judgment. But, in fact, a game is never actually won or lost in one or two dramatic plays or isolated decisions made by officials; the outcome depends on everything that happens from the beginning of the match (Stebbins 1987a, 151). Still, when it comes to "bad calls," players can lose their objectivity. Naturally, they can become even more incensed when an official is making bad calls throughout the game (to their disadvantage).

One source of tension unique to the individual sports is that of financial insecurity among junior professionals. Players must continually supplement inconsistent earnings from tournaments with such activities as teaching and endorsements. Theberge (1980) and Kutner (1983) report that junior females in golf and tennis defined the meagre income typically received at this point in their careers as a source of great tension. To be sure, salary negotiations can be stressful for team-based professionals, but this process is limited to certain periods of the year (usually pre-season) and is by no means a problem for everyone. In fact, the football players I studied never cited salary negotiations as a significant source of tension, although the matter was discussed in other contexts.

The tension over financial insecurity among professionals is as unsettling, if not more so, in the fine and popular arts. By way of evidence, the Canadian Government's Standing Committee on Communications and Culture (1989, 9) reports that the average net annual income for fine artists in Canada ranges from $11,079 for visual arts to $18,248 for musicians. The studies of magicians and stand-up comics suggest that the average remuneration is generally no better in the popular arts. Artists of all sorts are commonly forced to supplement their livelihoods with teaching or commercial applications of their art, or with wholly unrelated work. Several studies supply evidence regarding this point for fine artists (Sutherland 1989, 105–6; Wilson 1964, 26–8; Rosenblum 1978, 96; Adler 1975, 373; Stebbins 1968; Lacroix 1990; Cornwell 1979). Members of full-time symphony orchestras and repertory theatre companies enjoy a rare freedom from this occupational tension, as do the "stars" or leaders of each art.

Another source of stress for those in both the fine and popular arts is the onstage predicament: the possibility that things will go awry onstage and thus blemish the performance. Unfortunately, an unexpected incident that occurs during a performance or show can, if ineptly handled, alert the audience to the performer's momentary loss of control over the production. Because all hands are trying to realize a set of effects, the presentation and impact of which are managed by them, onstage predicaments are abhorred. This set of effects is what the audience has come to see. Unexpected and uncontrolled occurrences suggest that the performer is incompetent, an impression that he or she will go to great lengths to avoid. As bad an outcome is the tendency for such situations to destroy the performance's effect by diverting audience attention to a different reality.

For instance, a magician worries that a particular self-working trick may malfunction. A comic who uses audiotapes is concerned that the batteries in the tape player may run down. And as in all theatrical productions, potential onstage predicaments can emanate from the props. For example, one actress described how she fretted over the behaviour of a dog she had to carry around in one scene.

CONCLUSIONS

Despite the theoretical efforts of Homans, Thibaut, Kelly, and others, there is still no calculus in social psychology by which we can compute the motivational quotient of rewards over costs in amateur-professional pursuits. Nevertheless, it is possible to conclude, in accordance with Homans's proposition, that the amateurs and professionals considered in this book, after weighing the costs against the rewards, have found a "profit" in their work or leisure (see also Kelly and Ross 1989, 57 for further evidence). Therefore, they are motivated to continue the pursuit. I believe it is also safe to conclude, on the basis of the overall Project, that the cost-reward pattern of each field, and perhaps even its margin of profit, are unique. At the same time, this second conclusion in no way denies the observation made throughout this book: that certain types of costs and rewards exist in many, or all, of the fields examined here.

The profit of excess reward over cost is highly attractive. Nevertheless, although it was found that the rewards and thrills sometimes numerically surpass and always psychologically outweigh the disappointments, dislikes, and tensions, this way of measuring profit is still tautological. For this reason, profit was also measured by asking respondents such questions as whether they experienced an occasional craving to pursue their work or leisure (i.e., can they get enough), whether they would recommend it to their children, whether they planned to continue in it at the same or a higher rate of involvement, and whether they would choose another activity if they could start again. It was rare that a respondent considered reducing involvement, steering offspring away from the field, or starting again in a different field (for an exception, see Allison and Meyer 1988). In reality, many amateurs wanted more time for their serious leisure. Those who were spared this want were more fortunate; they alone were able to find the time to pursue their avocation at the pace they desired.

CHAPTER SEVEN

In the Community

Serious leisure and allied professional activities are greatly influenced by the social milieux in which they unfold. The results of the exploration of the marginality of amateur activities, undertaken in chapter 3, support this observation. Marginalization is a broad social process, wherein a group or an activity is set apart from related groups or activities, inside some larger social organization, such as an association or a community. The family is one sphere in which serious leisure is often marginalized.

FAMILY

The term "family" was used throughout the Project as an umbrella for all steady, adult relationships with a member of the opposite sex, whether or not children were present and whether or not the relationships were solemnized in a marriage ceremony. The children concerned were those conceived by the respondents. Given their age range of eighteen to eighty years or more, the amateurs were somewhat more likely than the professionals to be found in one of the relationships subsumed by this definition of family.

From the standpoint of participants in hot pursuit of an amateur or professional career, the boyfriend-girlfriend, or fiancé-fiancée, relationship was the least complicated and problematic of family ties possible. Here the partner usually tolerated or fully accepted the participant's passion for a particular art, sport, science, or field of entertainment. Given its centrality in the life of the latter, it is most likely that the former's rejection would be felt early in the formation of the relationship and hinder, if not completely terminate, its further development.

Rejection of the pursuit by the partner was a problem, however, for a minority of the respondents in sport and a somewhat smaller proportion in art and entertainment. Rejection also plagued married female barbershop singers significantly more than it did married male singers (Stebbins 1991). That is, some steady relationships, including a few marriages, ran aground in part, or in whole, because of one partner's enthusiasm for professional work or serious leisure. Some women were unable to identify with the sport in question (the baseball and football samples were all male); some found it unappealing; some found it was too demanding of their partner's time. Indeed, several wives tolerated their current situation only because they knew that their husbands had a limited number of playing years left before physical decline and removal from the game.

Travel, a main cause of relationship problems in entertainment, is something that comics undertake much more often than magicians. Hence, the former more than the latter reported both tolerance and rejection of their profession, sentiments typically sparked by loneliness and suspicions of infidelity while the entertainer is on the road. Moreover, it was male comics who reported these problems, for the females, although they travelled as well, were, with one exception, free of steady relationships. This, by the way, is largely a professional problem, for amateurs travel little in the entertainment fields I studied.

The only group for which I have data concerning family problems is that of theatre amateurs. Two marriages in the subsample of twenty-two married respondents broke up largely because of the artistic commitment of one person. In this art, the exclusiveness of interpreting and acting a major role produces family tension. The run of rehearsals, performances, and after-hours gatherings only adds to the growing estrangement from the partner, who seldom sees the amateur during this period.

Still, the overall conclusion is that immediate family members, including children, generally accept the amateur or professional pursuit that inspires the participant, despite the tension it can create (in the arts, see Lacroix 1990, 196–200). One reason is that older children and adult partners often see how meaningful the pursuit is for the person in question and, sometimes, even how it contributes to the community. Some family members even become directly involved in the pursuit, as seen with participating couples in music, theatre, archaeology, and astronomy. More indirectly, a spouse or child might help by cuing the family member who is learning a part for a play, or by serving as a "test" audience for a new magic trick that the member is working to perfect. Still more indirect, but very important, are the gestures of support of family members, whether that entails attending a participant's game, or performance, or working in an auxiliary capacity such as selling tickets (for amateurs), or keeping the books or promoting the act (for professionals).

Among the fields I studied, music and archaeology fostered the most family participation, both direct and indirect, whereas stand-up comedy and sport (football and baseball) fostered the least. It seems that it is the nature of the activity itself rather than the area of classification (i.e., art, science) that determines the form and extent of family involvement. Two broad conclusions are possible, however. First, the level of family involvement is inversely related to the level of family tension vis-à-vis the partner's serious leisure or professional work. Second, it is rare, indeed, that a person's amateur or professional pursuit meshes perfectly with the needs and interests of other family members.

The following poetic exchange between the wives of two amateur astronomers illustrates both the conflict and consensus that can emerge in amateur leisure.[1]

An Amateur Astronomer's Wife

I wake up with a start in the dead of the night,
I know something is wrong, and I turn on the light.
The place on the pillow beside me is bare,
My husband is missing, he's gone. Who knows where?
Perhaps he's recounting his variable stars,
Or seeing invisible markings on Mars.
When the moon is up high, and the earth's lights are dim,
Is he perched upon Plato's precipitous rim?
Oh, what is this thing that's come into our life?

There once was a time when my husband was mine,
Now he's way out in space where the galaxies shine.
And he spends all his time with his old telescope,
While I lie here alone, and I shiver and mope.
By the dawn he'll be back; as he grabs a few winks
He'll be dreaming of Venus, and Lepus, and Lynx.
And when he's awakened by coffee's sharp smell,
His eyelids will droop; he'll be grouchy, as well.
Oh, pity poor me, an astronomer's wife!

Mrs. Hedi E. Lattey

One Astronomer's Wife

I awake a few hours preceding the dawn
And find my astronomer-husband gone.

I bound out of bed – I cannot have this!
He's doubtless found something that I must not miss.
The moon, stars, and planets, the great nebulae,
Are worlds that my husband has opened for me.
Orion and Saturn are friends of us both,
Our telescope brings us a new means for growth.
What a wonderful thing has come into our life!

My husband, I note, is increasingly mine,
As together we go where the galaxies shine.
When he's perched upon Plato's precipitous rim,
He's not there alone – I accompany him.
At predawn and midnight, in front of our house,
I gaze into far distant space with my spouse;
And while at breakfast we both may be tired,
I'm elated in sharing new knowledge acquired.
Behold lucky me, an astronomer's wife!

Mrs. Lorena M. Cole

In a small, but still significant, proportion of relationships, the tension between an individual committed to a serious leisure pursuit and his or her partner with no such commitment appears to be a universal problem. Outside my own research, I have found casual observations about, and sometimes systematic data on, the problem in golf (Langton 1932), collecting (Gelber 1991), running (Robins and Joseph 1980; Krucoff 1990), wind surfing (Kamphorst and Giljam 1984, 26–7), and hang-gliding (Brannigan and McDougall 1987, 286–7). Yet, one should never lose sight of the fact that serious leisure can also lead to an amelioration of the participant's physical, psychological, and social well-being, which in turn can enhance family relationships. Strain in a relationship, moreover, is commonly caused by many factors, with commitment to a leisure activity being but one of them, possibly not even the most influential. Conversely, the leisure commitment can be seen as the most recent addition to a growing list of strains, the proverbial straw that breaks the camel's back.

WORK

In general, the occupations at which amateurs work during their non-leisure time are highly varied, with but one generalization possible: that there is no significant association between type of occupation or membership in a social class, and type of amateur pursuit. In other words, amateurs are employed in a variety of occupations, ranging from blue-collar through clerical, and on through professional, managerial, and executive. This proposition, which appears to hold for all serious leisure, is supported by this Project and the research of Finnegan (1989, 312), Bishop and Hodgett (1986, 37), Boothby and Tungatt (1978), Stebbins (1992), Carter (1975, 18–9), and Statistics Canada (1980).

Three points must be made with reference to this generalization. One, we are discussing the lack of an association between the occupations and social class of amateurs and their leisure pursuits, not the social-class background of their parents. At least in sport, there *is* evidence of a relationship between class background and the sport an athlete chooses (see McPherson, Curtis, et al. 1989, 176–9). Two, that background may influence the amateur's choice of an activity by allowing the individual to cultivate an interest in the activity while still in the family of orientation, obviously a possibility in certain amateur arts and sports (e.g., ballet, tennis) and certain hobbies (e.g., polo, art collecting). Furthermore, adequate financial resources are sometimes an important precondition to pursuing and succeeding in such activities, which suggests that money may be important, whether gained from family or work. Three, uncreative, mundane work may be especially likely to trigger a search for the phenomenon known as "psychological flow" (Csikszentmihalyi and Csikszentmihalyi 1988), which is available in serious leisure. Mitchell (1983, 191–2) found this predisposing condition in the lives of many applied scientists and similar professionals who are so prevalent in mountain-climbing circles. Apart from these caveats, however, the lack of an association between type of occupation, social class and serious leisure appears to hold for most amateur pursuits, many hobbies, and a wide range of volunteer roles. Of course, we are speaking of those who *work at an occupation*, not the *rentiers* at the top of the class structure or the dispossessed at the bottom. At these extremes, there may indeed be a relationship (see pp. 131–2 on unemployment and serious leisure).

As to the possibility of conflict between work and amateur pursuits, it is clearly infrequent. Amateurs try to avoid jobs that seriously interfere with their leisure. For instance, young athletes will likely seek work that leaves them free for baseball games on the weekend, and archaeologists may try to find work that allows for summer vacations and, hence, site-excavation trips.

Still, some serious leisure interests develop later in life, after an individual has entered an occupational career. Also, the career may have changed, such that it demands more time, available only from the sphere of leisure. In general, however, work comes first in any showdown. There is plenty of evidence from my own studies and those of others to support the proposition that amateur involvements (and those of the hobbyist and career volunteer, Stebbins 1992; Carter 1975, 30–5) often ebb and flow over the adult years. Individual participants struggle to balance work and leisure commitments with the condition of limited time ever in the background. Amateur activities usually take place during evenings and weekends, which accommodates the typical nine-to-five, Monday-to-Friday work schedule. As indicated earlier, this arrangement results in a full and hectic day for some participants, although at least they can have their leisure cake and eat it too, as it were. In short, leisure-work conflict is a problem for only a minority of amateurs.

Even where there is potential conflict, sympathetic employers often grant the amateur the time needed to play in a game or concert. For many employers, the donation of the occasional three or four hours away from the job poses few difficulties. Many, moreover, are sympathetic toward serious leisure; they see an affinity between it and the kinds of attitudes they want their employees to hold toward work, or between it and the approach they take to their own leisure. Perhaps they also sense long-term benefits for their own enterprise in these gestures of goodwill. Relatively uncommon are those employers who are unsympathetic or who oversee functions that allow little or no flexibility, such as when no substitutes can be found.

Looking at the other side of the coin – harmonizing work and amateurism – I found no consistent patterns. Instances of harmony can be found in every activity; usually they are expressed in a fundamental similarity between the person's work and his or her amateur pursuit, or in a flexible work schedule that facilitates participation in the leisure. One of the best examples was the interest of several professional engineers in developing the computerized automation of small telescopes; as amateur astronomers they are now using them to monitor the movements of binary and variable stars from remote sites (Hall, Genet, et al. 1986; Hays, Genet, et al. 1987). Other examples include the commercial artist who painted landscapes for enjoyment, the owner of a sporting goods store who played for an industrial league baseball team, and the saxophonist who repaired instruments by day and played in a jazz group on weekends. Although such an affinity between work and leisure clearly exists for some people, my observations suggest that most amateurs lack it to a significant degree.

Flexibility in performing one's job is a condition that aids some amateurs and not others. There are those who can take time away from their responsibilities to work on their avocation. For example, several respondents in the theatre study noted the necessity of sneaking a few minutes here and there to study a part. Occasionally amateur comics find their employment allows them sufficient time to write down, and perhaps even work on, ideas for developing a new monologue or improving an old one. Most work, however, neither facilitates nor hinders serious leisure. Mind you, amateurs in every field did say that they thought about their leisure activity while on the job. Thus, even if no active participation is possible, it can always provide a brief and pleasant diversion for those whose work allows the mind to wander from time to time.

AMATEURS AND PROFESSIONALS

Amateurs and professionals constitute a special part of each other's larger community. One aspect of this relationship was considered in chapter 3, where I described seven major links between the two categories and their publics. Now we turn to the nature of the interpersonal relationships across the four areas.

Late in this Project it became evident that sociological research on amateurism had advanced far enough to permit the following generalization:[2] relations between amateurs and professionals in the areas of art, science, sports, and entertainment are, depending on the area, *friendly, hostile, indifferent,* or *competitive.* Friendly relations prevail when members of these two groups join hands to carry out a common project, to find or administer an association or working unit, to participate in a teacher-student relationship, and the like. Hostility emerges when, for example, amateur activities encroach on the employment opportunities of professionals, or when those latter activities are defined as poor in quality, as a failure to meet the standards of excellence the best amateurs and professionals like to see guiding all work in their field. Indifference springs from isolation, from a lack of contact between amateurs and professionals. Usually, the professionals are only vaguely aware of the amateurs in their field, although the reverse is never true. Competitive relations pertain, however, when amateurs and professionals find themselves engaged in a contest against one another for a title or prize.

Although it is probably true that every field in the art, science, sports, and entertainment areas that has an amateur wing contains instances of all four types of relations, their prominence in any one field varies considerably. In sport, for instance, the general picture is one of indifference, even though sporadic cases of hostile, friendly, and competitive relations occur. Outside its recruitment arrangements, professional sport, for the most part, functions independently of its amateur counterpart. The code of non-remuneration prevents amateurs from becoming a threat in the labour market, and mediocre amateur play appears to have little effect on the spectators' opinions of professional efforts in the same sport. Outbreaks of hostility, as exemplified in the 1979 umpires' strike in baseball or the policy change by the Calgary Stampede that temporarily replaced professional rodeo cowboys with amateurs (Margoshes 1979), are too infrequent to alter the overall pattern of indifference. Contests involving amateurs and professionals, such as pro-am tournaments in bowling and golf, cannot begin to compete in significance with the spellbinding evolution of the baseball, basketball, football, and hockey seasonal standings, which culminate in widely ballyhooed playoffs.

Indifference also exists in science, but there is more hostility and friendliness, and competition is extremely rare. I found, for example, that many professional astronomers have little knowledge of or interest in the work of their amateur colleagues. Amateur inquiry has scant import for the specialities of these professionals. Other professional astronomers are hostile to some degree; they contend that amateurs do slipshod research or make a nuisance of themselves with incessant questioning. Some professional archaeologists and historians hold similar views (see also Turnbaugh 1983; Kelley 1963; Bisceglia 1980, 5). Yet, friendly relations also were noted in archaeology and astronomy. They formed, for instance, around mutual research projects and the professional conviction that some amateurs are capable of good work and of contributing to the advancement of their shared calling (see also Frison 1984; Gunter 1985; Zimmer 1990). Such cooperation also has been reported in history (Elton 1967; Finberg 1967, 44; Wall 1984), ornithology (Ainley 1980; Mayfield 1979; Mayr 1975, 376), mineralogy (Desautels 1969), and entomology (Watson 1975, 34).

Turning to the fine arts, indifference appears to be less prominent than in the preceding two areas. Professionals in the arts, more often than those in science or sport, are forced into some sort of association with amateurs. For example, it is common for them to teach to make ends meet. They may also be invited to perform for pay with amateur music or theatre groups that lack sufficient talent or numbers to produce creditable performances on their own (Maunsell 1963). This flow of talent is occasionally reversed, when professional performing units require assistance that only good local amateurs can economically provide. Casual observation suggests that friendly relations normally prevail under these conditions. Animosity arises, however, when professionals see their art endangered by second-rate amateur products (in music see, for example, *The New York Times* 1959, 9; Vaughn 1959; *Musical America* 1951, 11). Moreover, tempers have flared over the payment of amateurs when the work in question was seen by professionals as rightfully theirs (Parmenter 1962; Tomars 1964–66, 51–2; Seltzer 1989, 229).

Of the four main areas with amateur endeavours, it is entertainment that appears to have the lowest degree of professional indifference. The fuzzy distinction between amateur and professional and the routine practice of paid performance in both categories seem to make some kind of relationship – hostile, friendly, or competitive – inevitable. The studies of magicians and comics bear out this claim. Competition is generally highest in this area, partly because it lacks clear standards of excellence and effective mechanisms by which the professionals can control the entertainment market. Casual observation suggests that some amateur-professional competition exists, as well, in popular and commercial dance music. Tomars (1964–66, 51–2) has systematically observed such competition among painters.

THE WIDER COMMUNITY

Some of the groups studied have special public image problems that complicate their relations in the wider community. The arts, sports, and entertainment areas are plagued more by these problems than are the sciences. For instance, football players suffer from the stereotype of "dumb jock," or big and stupid men.[3] Stand-up comics are seen by the public as happy-go-lucky bohemians who make a great deal of money while indulging in the pleasures of sex, drugs, and alcohol. Magicians believe that they are publicly perceived, on the one hand, as mentalists capable of reading others' mind and, on the other, as entertainers who do not do "real work" (Prus and Sharper 1991, 250 and 294). Even the classical music students studied by Roberts (1991b) said they were seen by the public as "weird." In the theatre, Kohansky (1984, 3–11) speaks of the persistent image of the thespian as an immoral, sinister manipulator of human emotions. Zuzanek (1978, 3) describes the North American stereotype of fine artists in general, characterizing them as "intuitive, changeable, excitable, deep, interesting, and colourful, but also as outstanding individualists, radical and irresponsible and unwilling to contribute to the society in a disciplined way." In addition, artists are seen as making more money from their work than actually happens. Perhaps these views help explain the trend, observed in the United States, toward a decline in active participation in the arts (Kelly 1987, 54).[4]

In fields that have some degree of public appeal, namely those in sport and entertainment along with a few in fine art, the press has become a main conduit of fact and fiction about the practitioners. The public's image of certain types of athletes, entertainers, or artists is substantially based on indirect information, on what people read, hear, or see in the mass media. Reporters, being cut from the same cultural cloth as their audiences, are inclined to have a similar outlook. Thus journalistic accounts tend to reinforce the stereotypes described in the preceding paragraph.

From the scant scientific literature available on the mass media and public-centred professionals, it would seem that the audience is ready for a critical approach to the reporting of that group's activities. That approach, which may be less in vogue now than in the previous two to three decades, reports and analyzes flaws (as seen by journalists) in professional products and sometimes even in the lives of the professionals themselves (in sport, see Snyder and Spreitzer 1989, 256–7). Amateurs are spared this treatment. Indeed, the amateurs in every field studied in this Project complained that their activities were largely or wholly ignored by the media.

Meanwhile, many professionals have come to see the press as their occupational enemy number one, or at least as a force to be handled with great care. They see the press in two distinct roles: as critic (as just described) and as information agent. It is well known that professionals in art, sport, and entertainment dislike the opinions of the majority of journalistic critics, a sentiment that was explored in chapter 4.

Many professionals believe that journalists as information agents are people to be closely watched. They are held to have their own agendas, and their own idea of what constitutes news; what they are reporting is often, to the professionals' eyes, a distortion of the actual circumstances. Still, to the extent that professionals can control the flow of information to and through the press, or are confident that the press will evaluate their efforts favourably, they find it valuable as an avenue of publicity for themselves and their activities (in art see Rosenberg and Fliegel 1965, 208–14; Hanna 1988, 34–8; in sport see Snyder and Spreitzer 1989, 257–9). In other words, professionals in art, sport, and entertainment (and the amateurs, too, for that matter, e.g., Adler and Adler 1991, 86–92) are quite happy to cooperate with the media when it is to their advantage. On the whole, the professionals' sentiment toward critics, analysts, and similar agents is a mix of love and hate.

It should be mentioned that amateurs have image problems of their own. Among other definitions, standard dictionaries describe an amateur as a dilettante or dabbler, the epitome of which is Alexander Woollcott's assessment of the long-term fate of acting and prostitution: "The two oldest professions in the world – ruined by amateurs." On many occasions during the course of this Project, I have observed attempts to escape this image. Some groups changed their names, replacing the adjective "amateur" with something felt to be more benign. Seemingly less loaded descriptors were favoured, such as "non-professional" and "avocational"; or, in sport, "elite amateur." Amateurs, themselves, have felt the need at times to impress outsiders with the fact that they perform at professional or near professional levels. Members of amateur groups clearly know how to use amateur as both noun and adjective, which they do much as I have throughout this book. They also know that outsiders cannot always be trusted to do the same. Hence arises this special, at times awkward, relationship with the larger community that must be endured by amateurs.

Beyond the oftentimes fractious relations with the press and the discomforting images held by the public, lie a number of generally favourable involvements in the community, involvements that vary widely according to the field and area. In many cities, for example, astronomy clubs host an annual "star night," to which the public is invited to observe the evening sky through portable telescopes and, if available, a larger, permanently installed instrument. The event is typically run by experienced amateurs in collaboration with a professional or two. As well, some amateur and professional magicians and stand-up comics perform free of charge at certain charitable functions. Perhaps a professional athlete circulates in the community in several different capacities: as speaker at a high school sports banquet, prime attraction at the launching of a new business, or visitor at a camp for disabled children, among others. Some civic orchestras even supplement their regular performance schedules with a school concert or two. And university theatre professionals may work with high school drama clubs as advisers to the latter's productions. Common to all these jaunts into the wider community is the opportunity to interact with some of its members in the role of valued specialist.

In still broader terms, amateurism also contributes to the entire society, again in ways additional to those considered in the PAP system. Indeed, today amateurism is part of the broader spirit of participation sweeping contemporary postindustrial society. It has been serving in this fashion for many years. Barzun (1956a; 437) and Kaplan (1955, 4–6) have described how painting and music arose as mass activities in the 1930s in the United States, through government-sponsored orchestras, supplies, instruments, and lessons. Although the origin of the various amateur pursuits must be established separately in connection with the appearance of professionals in each, amateurism, generally speaking, extends back more than one hundred years. Mass amateurism, however, did bloom with the shortening of the workweek in this century.

Given that amateurs have been around in Europe and North America in smaller or larger numbers, for a long time, what contributions do they make to society? One such contribution is their help in building a unique ethos around their pursuit, which, in turn, helps attract new recruits as well as a larger, more enthusiastic public (in music see Drinker 1952, 577; Jackson 1967). Frye (1970) describes how ham-radio operators contributed to the electronic progress of the nation, as well as to the development in youth of an interest in professional electronics. These, he says, are of greater importance than the operators' communications in times of disaster or their contribution as trained operators to the military. In addition, persons outside the many PAP systems are encouraged through interpersonal ties to watch, view, or hear a performance or work of a friend or relative. In this manner, amateur and professional groups alike gather converts to their system, either as members of their public or as practitioners.

Toffler (1964) and Bell (1958, 185-9) see another contribution resulting from the upsurge of mass amateurism in the United States. Speaking particularly about the arts, Toffler (1964, 51-2) notes: "The rise of interest in the arts by a mass public in the United States could, despite all the tinsel and tomfoolery it entails, herald something quite important in the social development of modern man." In other words, when many people profit from amateur pursuits (and other serious leisure) through many or all of the nine rewards listed earlier (see pp. 94-5), the entire community profits from the resulting personal satisfaction. Perhaps if we were to *work as seriously* at our leisure as amateurs do (in those activities where serious work is possible), leisure might be less often described as a malady of contemporary Western civilization, as was Glasser's (1970, 190-2) wont.

Third, it is likely, as Albonico (1967) has suggested for university sports, that the many types of collective amateur activities contribute to communal and societal integration. This would seem to occur whenever people from different walks of life come together to engage in common leisure pursuits, before a public, and perhaps in competition with one or more other such groups (e.g., a national university basketball tournament, a touring community theatre group, a regional meeting of amateur archaeologists). Leisure, more effectively than work, promotes solidarity through the acquaintance and mutual understanding of individuals (Parker 1971, 56-7).

A final contribution of amateurism, and possibly the most far reaching, is its *salutary effect on the commonweal*. This, of course, is a main tenet in the ideology of every profession: that it contribute to the public good in a unique and beneficial manner. Because amateurs serve publics, often the same ones the professionals do, and because amateurs serve their allied professions through many routes, there can be no gain saying that they, too, benefit society by means of their activities.

Performing this sort of function only serves, once more, to point up their marginality, in contrast to those who partake of the more hedonistic popular leisure, which is believed to be destroying society. Kando (1980, 135–6) describes the pernicious effects of today's popular leisure on cultural life:

Our civilization's inability to translate gains in free time and money into leisure and the causes of this failure are ultimately rooted in the very fiber of our social system ... The dilemma is this: the same elements which were instrumental in creating the prerequisites for leisure – a materialistic and aggressive civilization able to develop technology and willing to use it – are now the obstacles to reaping the logical and beneficial outcome of these conditions ... As a consequence, with worldwide demand outpacing supply, we have sunk back toward scarcity. Thus, as circumstances keep international and individual life once again highly competitive, leisure is in as much jeopardy as ever.

MARGINALITY AND PARTICIPATION

I have been saying here and there in this book that amateurs are the marginal men and women of leisure, a statement that, although technically true, could lead to some theoretical confusion. They are not, for instance, the "marginal men" about whom Robert Park and Everett Stonequist wrote; that is, groups of people caught between two cultures. According to Park and Stonequist, those marginal people were often members of an ethnic minority whose marginality was a way of life that affected nearly every corner of their existence.

Marginality in leisure is hardly that pervasive. Rather, I got the impression over the course of this Project that amateurs are centrally located in many, perhaps all, of the other spheres of their lives; in family life, in work, in religion, and even in other areas of their leisure. Theirs is a segmented marginality.

Hence, the amateur is more accurately conceived of as occupying a marginal status, or a "marginal role" as Wardwell (1952) described it in his study of chiropractors. A marginal role is one that is incompletely institutionalized. There is ambiguity among its incumbents, and in the wider community, as to what the former should do and how they should behave. There are conflicting values and expectations, as well as incongruent status arrangements with professionals. Such roles are in the process of crystallization. They are common in industrialized societies, where rapid change spawns new occupations and new forms of leisure.[5]

I think "ambiguity" hits precisely at the heart of what is marginal about the status and role of modern amateurs. The amateurs' friends, relatives, workmates, and neighbours, on the one hand, are often in the dark about what they do and why they tend to pursue their activity with such passion (such matters were treated in chapter 3 under the headings of seriousness and uncontrollability). On the other hand, the professionals in the field understand perfectly well what the amateurs are doing. Yet amateurs and professionals differ over how many of the latter's functions should be attempted by the former. This Project brought a number of such ambiguities to light. For example, how much theoretical work should amateur archaeologists engage in? How often should amateur actors and actresses perform for pay? Should they be permitted to instruct theatre? Even in baseball, where the dividing lines are among the clearest, questions arise about using amateurs to pitch big-league batting practices. Indeed, the occasional semiprofessional status of amateurs is a source of concern, both to themselves and to professionals.

Amateurs are sometimes ambivalent about the pursuit of an avocation. Family, work, and leisure pull them in two, if not three, directions at once, making time demands that often far exceed the total available hours. In addition, there is an absence of community-wide institutional support for their leisure position, such as the support that helps sustain serious involvement in family and work activities. For example, such widely accepted values as providing well for one's family, being a hard worker or family oriented – all of which help to justify our efforts in these spheres – are simply lacking in amateurism. Moreover, their very existence in the institutions of family and work threatens amateur involvement elsewhere.

Most critical, however, is the fact that amateurs are marginal to the institution of leisure itself (on leisure as an institution, see Dumazedier 1971, 201–2; Kaplan 1975, 28–31; Kelly 1974, 137–9). That is, they implicitly or explicitly reject many of the values, attitudes, and patterns of behaviour that constitute leisure's very core. Like marginal people everywhere, they lack key institutional supports for their goals as well as their personal and collective ways of reaching them.[6]

Contributive participation summarizes both the spirit with which amateurs approach their avocational leisure and the effects of that activity on themselves, their allied professionals, and the community. Amateurs are first and foremost doers, rather than consumers of what someone else has done. They are proud of their active approach to leisure, while they disdain the passivity of, for example, steady television viewing. But, in participating in their avocation, they also contribute to the development of a science, the level of art in the community, or the availability of spectator sport. Perhaps as significant, amateurs contribute to themselves through the personal and social rewards of their avocation. In short, amateurism, as a serious leisure, offers important benefits.

This brings us to the question of creativity and marginality. It would be inaccurate to assert that amateurs, because they occupy a marginal role, are therefore creative. But it is possible that some creative people, including amateurs (most likely those in art, science, and entertainment), are also marginal. Edwards (1968, 448) states the case for marginality as a condition for at least some creativity: "But it does seem likely that the creative person – for reasons that are not yet understood ... is able to turn his marginal status, whether sought or unsought, to good advantage. Biographies of creative individuals suggest that marginality is usually a temporary episode in a creative career ... From a sociological point of view, the striking fact about such careers is the ability of creative individuals to alternate periods of disaffiliation and solitude with periods in which a variety of social roles are sustained with great effectiveness." It is doubtful that amateurs alternate between aloneness and gregariousness, but their marginality, restricted as it is to the sphere of leisure, may still foster among some a degree of creativity.

When compared with participants in casual leisure, amateurs are small in number but large in effect. It is for their many contributions to self and society that their activities truly merit the distinctive label of *avocation*; that is, a subordinate occupation pursued in addition to one's regular work. That avocation is the amateur's second calling.

CHAPTER EIGHT

Serious Leisure in the Twenty-first Century

In a partial review of American research into the sociology of leisure, Wilson (1980, 22–4) poses two crucial, interrelated, but as yet unanswered questions: Do people want more free, non-working time? And, is the amount of leisure time increasing? Let us turn to the first question.

The desire for more free time is a complicated issue. In the abstract, people want it, but their desire hinges upon certain conditions. For example, there must be no drop in income and fringe benefits. Mind you, if the economy is sound, living on even a modest reduction of wages as a trade-off for more non-working time is appealing.

Despite these conditions, a Canadian Gallup Poll (Canadian Institute for Public Opinion, 1986) showed that 45 percent of the sample was in favour of a shorter workweek, presented as four days (40 hours). In 1971, 34 percent supported this notion. But it may take many years for the five-day (40-hour) work schedule to die. Gill (1985, 172) reports resistance to its reduction in many westernized nations. There is also the suggestion that workers will not use the extra time for leisure, but instead will spend it tending to domestic chores or being with family (Veal 1987, 77).

Job sharing might allow additional time for leisure. A certain number of Canadians are apparently interested in this alternative (*Task Force on Employment Opportunities for the 80s*, 1982). But one American study of job sharing found that the time gained from this occupational arrangement is devoted chiefly to domestic obligations. Only 18 percent of those interviewed use the free time for leisure (Meier 1979, 45). Work in contemporary North America prevails over leisure, perhaps because people like work, identify with it, need the money, and hardly know how to use additional non-obligated time, or because they are influenced by some combination of these factors and other considerations.

Yet, turning to the second question, we note that many crystal-gazing scholars see a future containing increased leisure along with a reduced workweek (not just one that is compressed). They predict that people will eventually cease moonlighting and will reject many other obligatory activities that presently eat up non-work time. This change is occurring gradually; the average weekly hours of work for all workers in July 1990 were 34.7 in the United States and 31.7 in Canada (*Monthly Labor Review* 1990, 113; Statistics Canada 1990, 13–33). The average weekly hours of work are still near 40 in manufacturing and mining, however.[1]

Nonetheless, predictions still, as noted at the beginning of chapter 1, call for a sweeping reduction in the amount of time the average person will work. At the root of this trend is the technological revolution fostered by the microprocessor. Its ultimate effects are said to be shorter workweeks and fewer available jobs. Sherman (1986, 260) recommends that, to cope with the "new" industrial revolution, we reduce the length of the working lifetime. He further recommends that we provide opportunities for dignified and useful work for those so engaged, as well as financial security, so that such people, when not at work, can participate in interesting and substantial leisure activities.

From his observations, Newman (1983) concludes that attitudes toward work and leisure in Canada and the United States are changing in ways commensurate with Sherman's prescription for the good life. Newman lists five status symbols that he believes are becoming increasingly desirable as we move through the decade of the 1990s: a) self-directed free time, b) satisfactory balance of work and leisure, c) recognition as a creative person, d) rewards that are non-monetary, and e) commitment to community interests. Together these symbols form a constellation of values similar to that of the avocational entrepreneur presented in chapter 5. They also square with the mentality of the serious leisure participant in many lines of activity.

There will always be people who work. Some will do so because they find fulfilment in their jobs. The professionals of today and tomorrow tend to fall in this category; for many, the lines separating their work and leisure have always been imprecise. Other people will work as they do now, except for shorter periods on the job, because to them work is satisfying and interesting, even if it lacks the emotional investment of the ideal-typical professional calling. However, assuming that the high unemployment of the 1980s continues (Veal 1987, 176), the central life interest of many North Americans is likely to shift to the leisure segment of life, encouraging men and women to work only long enough to make the money needed to enjoy their free time.

LEISURE AS SOCIAL PROBLEM

The question that emerges with reference to a future blessed with more non-working time is how one is to find leisure activities that are interesting and substantial, worthy of becoming a central life interest. The lack of such leisure activities is becoming a major social problem for postindustrial societies. Indeed, to some extent, the problem is already upon us. E.M. Forster describes it in *A Passage to India*: "Most of life is so dull that there is nothing to be said about it, and the books and talk that would describe it as interesting are obligated to exaggerate, in the hope of justifying their own existence. Inside its cocoon of work or social obligation, the human spirit slumbers for the most part, registering the distinction between pleasure and pain, but not nearly as alert as we pretend."

In leisure, as in other difficult areas of life, we clearly suffer not from one problem but from many.[2] I shall concentrate here only on the challenge of conceptualizing how to achieve durable benefits from leisure in an age stressing evanescence. In chapter 1 we saw that durable benefits are gained from an activity (be it leisure or work), the conduct of which results in one or more of the following: self-actualization, self-expression, self-enrichment, re-creation or renewal of self, feelings of accomplishment, enhancement of self-image, social interaction and belongingness, and enduring tangible products of the activity (e.g., a painting or cabinet). Although these benefits do not necessarily last forever, they do last significantly longer than the evanescent benefits experienced by consumers of an activity that gratifies only in hedonistic ways. Some leisure pursuits appear to offer their participants a mixture of durable and evanescent benefits. Of course, durable benefits may include elements of hedonistic gratification, but the reverse – evanescent benefits having durable qualities – is probably empirically, and is certainly logically, impossible.

Sociologists disagree on the amount of contemporary leisure that can clearly be said to provide durable benefits. Dumazedier (1974, 42–3), for example, believes a new social norm has emerged that prescribes the use of leisure time to achieve personal fulfilment and self-expression. But others, such as Glasser (1970, 190–2), hold that we ought to pursue leisure of durable benefit, even though we presently tend to pursue only that of evanescent benefit. Support for the Glasser interpretation comes from the November 1986, Canadian General Social Survey (Parliament 1989), which collected data on how Canadians aged fifteen years and over spend a typical day. Nearly 23 percent of that day was devoted to leisure activities. Just over 53.5 percent of this leisure time was spent in the consumption of media communications, chiefly television, but also some radio, rented films, newspapers, and magazines. Activities capable of producing durable benefits for those who undertake them, classified in the survey as sports, hobbies, and voluntary activities, accounted for 18.3 percent of all leisure time. This figure, however, included respondents who dabble at these activities as well as those who treat them as serious leisure. The latter, my observations suggest, constitute a relatively small minority of the 18.3 percent. That survey, by the way, showed small variations for men and women employed outside the home and women working within the home.

One assumption underlying both positions is that the leisure returning only evanescent benefits – most mass or popular leisure – is a low-yield use of free time. The implication is that such time could be spent in more personally rewarding ways, by taking part in activities that are self-actualizing, self-enriching, re-creative, and the like.

I propose the pursuit of serious leisure – composed of amateur, hobbyist, and career volunteer activities – as the remedy to help solve the social problem of meaningless or empty leisure. In part, the conceptualization just sketched both confirms and helps explain the assorted adages: that one gets out of an activity that which one puts into it; that little effort returns little benefit and great effort returns great benefit. For example, developing oneself as an athlete, actor or scientist requires – among other activities – long hours of practice, conditioning, and studying. But, in undertaking such activities, one also realizes, or begins to realize, one's athletic, artistic, or intellectual potential; the durable benefit is self-actualization, which satisfies an important need (Maslow 1954). Similarly, socially valued personal qualities gained through steady effort are more apt to bring greater public approbation (when manifested on playing field or stage, or in learned journals) than are the more superficial, comparatively easily attained qualities found among those performing for a small circle of participants, such as the playing of a simple line in a family music ensemble or the performing of a self-working trick as a magician. Moreover, once having struggled to reach an effective level of artistic, athletic, scientific, or entertainment skill or knowledge, the amateur or hobbyist is in a position to repeat experiences that will never be available to people without such skill or knowledge. For instance, only those astronomers who own sufficiently powerful telescopes (very likely ones they made themselves) and have a knowledge of how to use them to "find their way around the sky" are in a position to experience a star's lunar occultation or the fluctuation in light of a distant variable star. Clearly, feelings of accomplishment are more likely to be intensified and self-conceptions strengthened when preceded by a major, rather than a minor, effort.

Finally, activities that demand exceptional output from their participants and produce feelings of accomplishment, enhanced self-image,
or tangible products, not to mention some of the other durable benefits
discussed here, also tend to produce that certain "flow" (Csikszentmihalyi 1988, 29–35) in which the participant is completely involved with
the activity. Being totally absorbed leaves little time or inclination for
thoughts of other matters. What better way is there to renew oneself
after a day in the office, shop, or kitchen?

LEISURE IN RETIREMENT

Leisure is possibly most problematic for the retired or unemployed
segment of society. They, more than those faced with obligatory
responsibilities, have time on their hands. Furthermore, it would seem
that leisure is an important consideration if the retirees, or unemployed
people, want to continue to realize the non-monetary benefits they
enjoyed during employment.

There are numerous serious leisure activities of interest to the elderly
that can be taken up at retirement or expanded at that point, having
been developed earlier. In the arts, there is music, theatre, painting,
and sculpting; in sport (and games), golf, tennis, bowling, and chess;
and in science, entomology, local history, archaeology, astronomy,
mineralogy, and ornithology. There are hobbies such as bridge, collecting, barbership singing, shuffleboard (Snyder 1986), and knitting,
along with innumerable volunteer activities. Some of these carry physical requirements that limit participation; some exact a lengthy period
of preparation before participation becomes significantly rewarding.
But all include among their enthusiasts men and women in their
middle fifties and older.

So far, I have been able to identify seven functions of serious leisure
in the lives of the elderly: providing worklike activity; offering a
possible link with one's former work associates and current friends and
relatives; expanding one's social circle; promoting transcendence; constituting a theme in the life review; fostering responsiblity; and meeting
certain needs of other people. Several of these functions emerged
after my interviews with, and observation of, twenty-two amateurs
(approximate ages: 55–84 years) engaged in magic, archaeology,
astronomy, and theatre. Further observational and library research
was conducted with regard to classical music amateurs, many of whom
were retired. Unruh's (1983) study of the social worlds of the elderly
provides additional data on these seven functions.

Serious leisure is a worklike activity in the sense that, like many jobs,
it is challenging and valued by someone (i.e. the public); it also contains

a status system and generates a set of colleagues. Retirees whose former occupational careers were rewarding for these reasons could, if they came into contact with an attractive avocation, continue to enjoy such rewards throughout much of their remaining life. The previously mentioned forms of serious leisure all require some combination of skill, knowledge, and talent for satisfactory involvement. Thus, the stage is set for the development of status systems founded on gradations of excellence. An appealing social identity and self-image are available to those participants – retired or not – who strive to excel and who are recognized by their associates for having done so.

Many serious leisure participants, of course, are committed to their fields long before occupational retirement overtakes them. Especially in sport, vocational colleagues develop into avocational colleagues as well. To the extent that all concerned maintain their common leisure interests, a link is thereby forged between retirees and their work associates (retired or still employed). Similar ties are established with friends and relatives in the community (including children and grandchildren, my data suggest) through shared leisure interests. Indeed, one of the remarkable aspects of every serious leisure activity I have studied so far is the wide range of ages (middle teens to over eighty) in the local groups.

Many retired people decry the loss that accompanies the termination of work and the death of close friends (Roadburg 1985, 147–8). Serious leisure pursuits help offset this tendency, by offering formal groups and informal networks of devotees with whom the aged can share their interests. Moreover, these circles are typically heterogeneous in terms of age, education, religion, former or current occupation, and the like. Here is an appealing diversity that social clubs for the elderly seldom provide (Ashton 1971).

It is possible that some serious leisure participants may even garner a sense of "transcendence" or "symbolic immortality" from their avocation endeavours (Gaev 1976; Lifton 1977). Indeed, worthwhile contributions, such as paintings, scientific journal articles, recorded musical performances, or remarkable volunteer service, may outlive those who produce them. Although the idea of transcendence is normally applied to occupational achievement, there is no reason to exclude meritorious avocational achievement that endures, in some public way, beyond the producer's lifetime. Admittedly, the danger exists that, like the unsung poet in Milton's "Elegy in a Country Churchyard," some amateur or hobbyist efforts will not only fail to gain immortality, but even fail to attract public attention while their creators are living. Serious leisure, like a job, carries with it the possibility of failure.

Participants who do accomplish something of significance during their lifetime, whether or not it is transcendent, have a basis for self-respect. In fact, avocational achievement is the most noteworthy expression of ability for some, since neither their domestic nor occupational routines offer similar opportunities. For the elderly, it is during the life review that these leisure achievements take on special meaning. According to Butler (1977, 330), the "life review [is] a naturally occurring, universal mental process characterized by the progressive return to consciousness of past experiences and, particularly, the resurgence of unresolved conflicts; simultaneously, and normally, these revived experiences and conflicts can be surveyed and reintegrated." Serious leisure accomplishments thus give the individual something that can be retrospectively viewed with pride.

One of the disheartening aspects of old age is the declining level of responsibility that attends it (Riley, Foner, et al. 1988, 280). Other people encroach on the everyday decision making of the elderly, committing them to an increasingly dependent existence. We saw, however, that amateurism, particularly that in the sciences, promotes the leisure lifestyle of the avocational entrepreneur, where initiative, independence, and responsibility for one's own success and failure are the *modus operandi*. Furthermore, amateurs, even the individualist entrepreneurs, are usually connected with organizations of one sort or another, which are run by the amateurs themselves. The assistance so often needed in administering these groups can be supplied by the retired person, who, potentially, has more time available.

The growing desire of many old people to serve the needs of others, rather than simply become the object of their service, is related to this declining responsibility. Although certain types of volunteer work might satisfy this desire better than any amateur or hobbyist pursuit, the fact that amateurs and hobbyists everywhere serve some sort of public should not be overlooked. When participating in a scientific project, an artistic performance, or an athletic contest, the practitioner is making a contribution that is appreciated by someone. In addition, skilled or knowledgable amateurs and hobbyists sense their relative indispensability; practitioners as good as they are are hard to find. Many types of career volunteers develop a similar outlook.

Rewards of Serious Leisure

Serious leisure, with its interweaving of skills, knowledge, and talent, is most rewarding when the participant has been able to develop these three to an admirable degree. Hence, it is obviously to the advantage of any would-be participant to enter the pastime before – in fact long before – retirement. As Mulac (1977) notes: "If one has never learned to enjoy leisure in one's youth, early adult, or middle years, how can one be sure that it will suddenly and miraculously be enjoyable in retirement." Many people reach later life completely unprepared for the increased leisure available to them (Godbey, 1990, 160).

Getting started in serious leisure early in life also enables one to acquire, while one has the income, the necessary resources and training. Indeed, the reduced income of many retirees may prevent the most effective pursuit of an avocation. They simply lack the money to buy a good telescope or musical instrument, high-quality paints and brushes, or regular piano lessons.

There are serious leisure fields, however, where little or no monetary outlay is required. The theatre is typically one of these; others include chess, bridge, and archaeology. Unless one joins an exclusive club, tennis is also relatively inexpensive. Certain areas of ornithology, mineralogy, and local history, collecting, and volunteering can all be enjoyed with minimal financial commitment.

Most importantly, participants must find in their chosen avocation many of the durable benefits mentioned earlier. Serious leisure is the only sphere in modern leisure where these rewards can be systematically sought and experienced.

LEISURE IN UNEMPLOYMENT

A main tenet of Marxian thought is that capitalism inevitably creates a significant level of unemployment, an inherent contradiction in this type of economy. Marx argued that, in capitalistic enterprise, owners try to employ ever more efficient means of production as a way of increasing profits. Mechanization, automation, and, recently, computerization have been among the main routes to the intertwined goals of profit and efficiency. But as these vast changes spread through industry and industrialized society, they leave periods of unemployment in their wake. These are the adjustments occasioned by the new jobs those changes have created and the old ones they have eliminated. Marxists argue further that the choice of leisure, whether during unemployment or after working hours, is, in reality, no choice at all. Instead, they claim, workers are paid by capitalists, given sufficient leisure time to replenish their energy and then subtly directed to use their money to buy in a market of capitalist goods and services, including those available in the leisure sphere. An individual's social class, a structure created by the conflict between capital and labour, they say, determines the kinds of leisure the person will participate in.

Another way of interpreting this contradiction is to say that it forces the expansion of non-obligatory time, time gained by default because of lack of work. Following the Marxist line of thought, we might then ask if, generally speaking, forced non-obligated time is any more or less monotonous than forced work. After all, a number of authors have noted that most of the means provided by modern technology are passive, non-involving, and non-creative (e.g., Czurles 1976; Iso-Ahola 1980). Given that both work and leisure rely heavily on these means, could the level and extent of monotony not be the same in both spheres? As to how monotonous either is, that depends on its nature. Just as some work is monotonous (e.g., assembly-line work, manual labour), so might some leisure be as well (e.g., sitting idly wishing for more interesting things to do, watching television for lack of an appealing alternative). Unemployment, like retirement, is a clear manifestation of forced non-obligated time. Can an individual find stimulating, or true, leisure, whether casual or serious, in such circumstances?

The minimal research on this question offers a confused picture. Gelber (1991) reports that hobbies enjoyed considerable popularity during the Great Depression in the United States. Shamir (1985), in a study carried out in Israel of unemployed men and women with university degrees, found that those with a strong Protestant ethic and work involvement were much more likely to turn to, and benefit from, leisure activities than those with a weaker ethic. Tess (1990), who studied a small, racially mixed subsample of men and women in Britain who had developed interests in certain serious leisure activities while unemployed, found that whereas, for them, the experience of unemployment was positive, for the majority of unemployed people in her main sample, it was not. Despite their lack of paid work, those people in the subsample had sufficient money to sustain life and participate in their leisure, especially when compared with those in the overall sample. The subsample members were also more self-confident. Tess (1990, 415) reviewed several other studies reporting a positive link between leisure participation and a reduction in the psychological depression created by unemployment. But she concludes that, most of the time, this link never develops:

In practice, however, the increase in non-work time which unemployment brings seldom translates into an increase in leisure. In many ways, unemployment and leisure are fundamentally incompatible: while "leisure" is regarded as pleasurable, freely chosen activity, the experience of unemployment is rarely pleasant; the unemployed seldom feel free to use their time as they please, and the depression and lethargy which afflict them discourage their participation in activities. When they are out-of-work, few unemployed people develop a leisure-based lifestyle, for the underlying flaw in the argument for a leisure solution to the problems of the unemployed is that it is simply very difficult for people who have been demoralized by unemployment to motivate themselves to construct a lifestyle based on leisure activities. The burden of sustaining these activities may increase, rather than relieve, the stresses of the unemployed.

The lesson to be learned, here, is that sitting around with nothing to do is no more an instance of true leisure than of true work. Both work and leisure are purposive, designed to achieve some sort of end. Unemployment frees the worker from the job. But sitting around is *marginal* leisure; it can become true leisure only when sought after. Determination, enthusiasm, and sometimes financial resources must be present for true leisure to develop. The choices made when these psychological and economic conditions are met are, to be sure, constrained by class and culture, by various power relations as Rojek (1987) has put it. Within these broad limits, however, the aforementioned studies suggest that serious leisure, rather than casual leisure, is what varying, albeit small, proportions of the unemployed find and enjoy.

Notwithstanding the pessimism concerning the possibility of finding true leisure while unemployed, a number of analysts (e.g., Fisher 1976; Dawson 1986) have suggested that we educate for unemployment. Typically that includes some reference to instruction or training in leisure. Unemployment is now seen as a natural and permanent part of capitalism, for which people must be prepared. People should learn, for example, to participate in serious leisure through courses in the arts and humanities, training in sport, or recruitment for volunteer roles. Of note, here, is the fact that Marx himself saw art as a liberating activity, as a form of human expression that works independently of the cultural hegemony that dominates the mind in the capitalist workplace. Is it not possible, then, that the non-artistic forms of serious leisure might be just as liberating, inasmuch as they often require the same kinds of initiative, independence, and inventiveness?

The studies in this Project, and the grounded theoretic generalizations that have emerged along the way, are theoretically distant from the macrosociological Marxian propositions dealing with cultural hegemony, social class domination, and capitalist exploitation. These latter ideas pertain to entire societies or great parts of them, whereas the studies and generalizations in this book flow from the ethnographic tradition in sociology and anthropology, which centres on the everyday experiences of local groups of people and what can generally be said about them. Yet, analyses of leisure and unemployment, both

Marxian and non-Marxian, tend to ignore, as does much of the rest of social science, the serious forms of leisure masked by the swirl and "hype" of casual leisure. We now, however, have evidence, micro-sociological to be sure, that serious leisure sometimes fails to square with the macrosociological claims of the Marxists.[3] It seems that class, with the exceptions noted in chapter 7, is rarely a barrier to participation in much of serious leisure. In reality, people in many walks of life have the money (at times, it is a condition for participation) and the interest to pursue an attractive hobby, volunteer role, or amateur activity.

I remain convinced that serious leisure is an important antidote to the dreary state of being unemployed. I remain equally convinced that serious leisure, because it demands consistent effort, devotion, and some hardship, will be shunned by a significant proportion of the adult population, be they employed, unemployed, or retired. But until many people become aware of and sample the possibilities offered by serious leisure, social scientists will continue to be ignorant about the nature and extent of its appeal, whatever the constraints imposed by class and whatever the debilitating effects of unemployment. At any rate, it is time to bring serious leisure – the best kept secret of modern times – down from the attic.

Conclusion

With this discussion of serious leisure in the twenty-first century, I have come to the end of my fifteen-year Project and related studies, together with my development of a formal grounded theory. Of course, much research remains to be done, the Project having raised many more questions than it answered. But that is the nature of scientific exploration. It helps to chart new intellectual territory, so that others may better examine it. It also gives fellow travellers an idea of where to go and, once there, what data collection tools to use.

Studies now beckon on all fronts. For example, we should be looking at the various kinds of careers pursued by serious leisure participants, as well as the different patterns of their attendant costs and rewards. I have felt all along – given my long-standing penchant for social psychology, in general, and symbolic interactionism, in particular – that my examination of the social organization of serious leisure was not as thorough as my exploration of its cultural and interactive bases. To be sure, chapters 7 and 8 did address a number of community- and societal-relationships, but there is still much to learn at this level, especially regarding unemployment and retirement. Even the basic descriptions and definitions of amateur, professional, hobbyist, and career volunteer will undergo modification as we delve deeper into these spheres of life.

At present, the most poorly understood of all the facets of serious leisure is, without doubt, its various publics. The comparatively small number of pages in chapter 4 itself attests to this deficiency. Whatever one's research and theoretical bent – macrosociological or microsociological, quantitative or qualitative – the scope is now wide open for new data as well as ideas concerning precisely who the various publics are and how they fit into their respective PAP or HP systems.

Finally, let me close with the exhortation that this is the moment for a careful consideration of the relationship between casual and serious leisure, now that the territory of the latter has been reasonably well staked out. In fact, I have treated casual leisure as a residual category throughout this book, describing and defining it only to the degree necessary to set it off from its more serious counterpart. Indeed many more people still pursue the first rather than the second category of leisure activity; even dyed-in-the wool serious-leisure participants occasionally seek out time in which simply to relax. Casual leisure, moreover, has already been widely studied, although rarely in direct comparison with serious leisure. Nonetheless, by using each as a comparative backdrop for the other, we should be able to learn a great deal about both types.

There it is: the gauntlet is down. Let us make sure that serious leisure has a prominent place on the research agenda of the next century. Only then will we begin to discover what it really can and cannot do for the human condition.

Notes

1 The closest sociology had come to a definition was available in an article by Elizabeth Todd (1930), a largely historical discussion about the emergence of amateurism in modern times.

CHAPTER 1

1 Under the assumption of a modestly growing economy, projections are for an overall increase in jobs (e.g., *U.S. Bureau of the Census*, 1988, 325).

2 Compared with casual leisure, the serious variety has received scant research attention. To the extent that this research bears on the scope of this book, much of it is reviewed here. Although they have generally shunned serious leisure as a research topic, a few scholars (e.g., de Grazia 1962, 332–6; Glasser 1970, 190–2; Kaplan 1975, 80, 183; Kando 1980, 108) have recognized the distinction between serious and casual leisure (they use different adjectives however). De Grazia, Glasser, and Kaplan lean toward the former as the ideal way for members of post-industrial society to spend their discretionary time.

3 Whether some collectors are hobbyists or amateurs will eventually be decided by research on the professionalism or lack of it among full-time curators of various kinds of collections.

4 Indeed, historical writings about amateurs, when centred on the pre-professional phase of a field of leisure, are actually about the gentlemen amateurs of the day who, according to the present framework, are more accurately classified as hobbyists. Only in retrospect, by comparing the earlier hobby with its subsequent professional development, can we refer to them now as amateurs.

5 The scope of career volunteering is even broader than this, for Statistics Canada incorporates "other" categories throughout its publication, thus

suggesting that this type of serious leisure is, at present, difficult to classify completely.

6 For a discussion of volunteering as a career, see Floro (1978, 197–8).

7 It may happen, especially in social action and in advocacy and political groups, that senior volunteers in the organization tell the junior ones what to do. And volunteer boards of directors may delegate, in a general way, certain tasks to paid executives within the organization.

8 Delegated tasks are different from the tasks carried out by amateurs in such collectivities as theatre companies and community orchestras. Amateurs try out for their roles or chairs in these groups, all of which are reserved for group members, for *insiders*. In other words, whereas there would be no group were it not for the amateurs, groups using volunteer help could survive and function without it, albeit often less effectively. Moreover, the tasks of such amateurs are usually ones the leader is unable to carry out (for example, no conductor plays every instrument in the orchestra); hence they are not delegated in the sense used here to describe volunteer tasks.

CHAPTER 2

1 By stressing the professional references made in the dictionary definitions of amateur, I am simultaneously and arbitrarily ignoring the pejorative references of "inexperienced," "incompetent," "dabbler," and the like also made there. Both conceptions are prevalent. But a single scientific concept cannot contain such opposites. One must choose. Dabbler is the label given in chapter 3 to the category of non-professional, part-time participant with these unflattering characteristics.

2 There are 168 hours in a week. If, in a typical week, a person devotes 40 of them to work and work-related obligations and 74 to sleep and body maintenance (existence time), 54 hours remain for leisure and non-work obligations. Although activities defined as obligations (e.g., going to the cleaners, grocery store, service station) reduce this discretionary time still further, many people are still left with about as much time for pure leisure as for work. There are, of course, atypical weeks, when all these proportions expand or contract, leaving more or less time than usual for pure leisure, during which enjoyment is routinely expected and sought.

3 Specifically, these data come from interviews with, or participant observation of, magicians, astonomers, football players, and stand-up comics. Studies of public-centred professions that directly consider the question of professionalism there are rare. Instead, it is common to assume professional status in these areas. A small number of studies have, however, provided support, in one way or another, for one or a few of the professional attributes of, for example, soccer players

(Roadburg 1976), jazz musicians (Buerkle and Barker 1973), cp. 3–5), dancers (Perreault 1988), ornithologists (Ainley 1980), astronomers (Lankford 1981a), scientists (Zuckerman and Merton 1971), female golfers (Theberge 1980), female tennis players (Kutner 1983), actors (Kohansky 1984, 3–11), photographers (Schwartz 1986), and fine artists (Freidson 1983b).

4 To be sure, a dying patient would most likely be keenly interested in a recent medical breakthrough that promises a cure for his or her illness. What is being argued here is that that same patient would take little real interest in past breakthroughs that are now part of the taken-for-granted, routine treatment of the illness.

5 Roadburg (1976) found that British soccer players used similar criteria to define themselves as professionals.

6 The disarray in the sociology of professions is nowhere more apparent than in its attempts to define its central concepts. Here, there is currently even disagreement on how much agreement there is on definitions. Forsyth and Danisiewicz (1985, 59) argue that there is *no* agreement on definitions of key concepts in this area.

7 I am not suggesting in this comparison that we conceive of it only in terms of a continuum as Greenwood (1957) did. An ideal-typical analysis can reveal many different kinds of relationships. We might discover, for instance, that professions and all other occupations have a bipolar relationship to each other with reference to some or all of the attributes, or that a given attribute is found in all occupations to more or less the same degree.

CHAPTER 3

1 It should be evident from this example that, although professionals tend to set and communicate the standards, they sometimes fail to meet them.

2 Even people employed professionally in a field outside their avocation manage to sustain consistent, active involvement in that avocation. There are doctors' symphonies in New York, St. Louis, Los Angeles, and Boston. A businessmen's symphony operates in Chicago. Occupations known for their long hours of work, such as self-employment, high-level management, and the professions, were well represented among the amateurs in six of the eight field studies. The sports teams observed were composed of young men, most of whom were not yet well established in work careers. Nonetheless, such sports as tennis, golf, squash, and racketball appear to be attractive as serious leisure for many people with extensive work commitments.

3 Kaplan (1955, 12) equates lack of skill and knowledge with amateurism which, of course, fails to square with the argument tendered here.

Although amateurs are often less skilled than professionals, the differences in skill are a matter of parallel gradation.

4 In this paragraph, my development of a sociological definition of "amateur" takes an arbitrary turn. Whereas novices and dabblers are occasionally treated as synonymous with amateurs in everyday usage, I am clearly distinguishing between them.

5 The empirical cutting points used throughout the Project between devotee and participant are always peculiar to each pursuit, there being no better way to make the distinction than to use criteria found among and understood by its participants. Thus disagreements are possible, such as between my own classification of astronomers and that of Thomas R. Williams (1987), who distinguishes between amateur astronomers (contributing scientists), observing astronomers (non-contributing hobbyists), and armchair astronomers (readers of astronomy).

6 Etzkorn (1973, 196), drawing on the later writings of Paul Honigsheim, notes a similar form of recruitment of professional musicians from amateur organizations in Germany and Russia.

7 This is the participants' view. The average member of their public, being neither amateur nor professional, may enjoy a performance or a product that pleases the participants somewhat less because, by the participants' criteria, it is substandard.

CHAPTER 4

1 Science is the exception here, where by far the largest proportion of the public is normally collegial (Woolgar 1988, 89).

2 Obviously, this does not apply to some elite amateur sports and sports events.

CHAPTER 5

1 The concept of scientist as entrepreneur being developed here is different from that of entrepreneurial scientist, or someone who turns his or her scholarly products into saleable products for personal or institutional profit (see Etzkowitz 1989).

2 This is not an attempt to liken amateur scientists to tradesmen. In everyday usage, these three terms are applied to any field where extensive knowledge and ability must be developed before independent practice is possible.

3 All amateurs, apprentices included, are aware of the possibility of accidentally discovering something new. But even apprentices observe or do fieldwork chiefly for other reasons, realizing how rare such discoveries are.

CHAPTER 6

1 The rewards were initially derived inductively. In the interviews, amateurs, and later professionals, identified the various aspects of their pursuits that they found appealing. As the list stabilized, I began to administer it on a card, asking respondents to rank, from most to least important, all the rewards relevant to them.
2 The use of the noun "enjoyment" is in line with the distinction Podilchak (1989) drew between it, a self-oriented process, and "fun," a socially oriented one. My earlier writings generally treated fun in the enjoyment sense.
3 The professional astronomers were never asked about the rewards of their work.
4 Put another way, such generalizations as are possible to make are too broad to be scientifically useful. One could note, for instance, that there are career-related disappointments in art, sport, and entertainment, but this statement tells us little about their nature.
5 Rare was the mention of how disappointing it is to be cut from a team. This was partly due to sampling procedure, for I studied only those who "made" the team. Moreover, being cut often means the end at that level of competition. It is a one-time disappointment, unlike failing an audition in the fine or popular arts, after which the performer has many other parts or positions to try out for.

CHAPTER 7

1 *Sky and Telescope* 18 (1958):87; 18 (1959):137.
2 This passage, from Stebbins (1987b, 93–5) has been modified.
3 There are, of course, exceptions. Donnelly and Young (1985, 27) note that North American rugby players are rather fond of their public image as drunken brawlers.
4 Hobbyists are not immune to negative images, as Stenross (1990) points out with reference to hunters, shooters, and gun collectors.
5 Role marginality is different from status inconsistency, a term that refers to incongruent requirements among two or more already crystallized roles. A substantial degree of role clarity is necessary for the inconsistencies to be apparent.
6 As near as I can tell, the idea of marginality has received little attention from students of serious leisure and the public-centred professions. At least there is very little reference to the notion anywhere except in art, where Judith Blau (1988, 274) has summarized a small literature on the alienation and marginality of the professional artist. I have also examined the marginality of hobbyist barbershop singers (Stebbins 1991).

CHAPTER 8

1 This pattern holds despite time-budget data indicating that Americans increased their leisure by about 10 percent between 1965 and 1975 (Robinson and Godbey 1978). It is possible that this gain was made largely by salaried workers, whose hours of employment are not reflected in hourly rated wage-earner averages. Or it may be a product of reduced non-work obligations.
2 One related leisure problem is that of unequal distribution of free time in industrial societies. Some gainfully employed people have much more of it than others (White 1982).
3 Indeed, Wilson's (1988, 61–9) review of the relationship between class and leisure discloses numerous instances in which the working class has rejected certain mainstream cultural artifacts and symbols, as well as certain mainstream leisure patterns. There is less upper-class or capitalist influence here than is claimed in theory.

Bibliography

Abbott, Andrew. 1988. *The System of Professions*. Chicago: University of Chicago Press.

Adler, Judith. 1975. "Innovative Art and Obsolescent Artists." *Social Research* 42:360–78.

Adler, Patricia, and Peter Adler. 1987. *Membership Roles in Field Research*. Beverly Hills, Calif.: Sage.

Adler, Patricia, and Peter Adler. 1991. *Backboards and Blackboards: College Athletes and Role Engulfment*. New York: Columbia University Press.

Adler, Peter, and Patricia Adler. 1982. "Championing Leisure: The Professionalization of Racquetball." *Journal of Sport and Social Issues* 6:31–41.

Ainley, Marianne G. 1980. "The Contribution of the Amateur to North American Ornithology: A Historical Perspective." *Living Bird* 18:161–77.

Albert, Edward. 1984. "Equipment as a Feature of Social Control in the Sport of Bicycle Racing." In *Sport and the Sociological Imagination*. Ed. Nancy Theberge and Peter Donnelly. Fort Worth, Tex.: Texas Christian University Press.

Alberta Recreation and Parks. 1990. "Volunteerism in the Recreation Sector." *A Look at Leisure*, no. 27 (February).

Albinson, John G. 1976. "The Professional Orientation of the Amateur Hockey Coach." In *Canadian Sport*. Ed. Richard S. Gruneau and John G. Albinson. Don Mills, Ont.: Addison-Wesley Canada.

Albonico, R. 1967. "Modern University Sport as a Contribution to Social Integration." *International Review for Sport Sociology* 2:155–64.

Allison, Maria T., and Carrie Meyer. 1988. "Career Problems and Retirement of Elite Athletes: The Female Tennis Player." *Sociology of Sport Journal* 5:212–22.

Altheide, David L., and Erdwin H. Pfuhl, Jr. 1980. "Self-Accomplishment through Running." *Symbolic Interaction* 3:161–77.

Altheide, David L., and Robert P. Snow. 1979. *Media Logic*. Beverly Hills, Calif.: Sage.

Andrews, Donald S. 1981. "Socializing Agents and Career Contingencies Affecting the Elite Hockey Player during His Active and Post-Active Occupational Career." *Arena Review* 5:54–63.

Aran, Gideon. 1974. "Parachuting." *American Journal of Sociology* 80:124–52.

Ashton, E.T. 1971. *People and Leisure*. London: Ginn.

Bain, Wilfred C. 1967. "The University Symphony Orchestra." In *The American Symphony Orchestra*. Ed. Henry Swoboda. New York: Basic Books.

Ball, Donald W. "Failure in Sport." 1976. *American Sociological Review* 41: 726–39.

Barrell, Garry, Audrey Chamberlain, John Evans, Tim Holt, and Jill Mackean. 1989. "Ideology and Commitment in Family Life: A Case Study of Runners." *Leisure Studies* 8:249–62.

Barthes, Roland. 1975. *Roland Barthes*. London: Macmillan.

Barzun, Jacques. 1954. "The Indispensable Amateur." *Juilliard Review* 1:19–25.

– 1956a. "New Man in the Arts." *American Scholar* 25:437–44.

– 1956b. *Music in American Life*. Bloomington: Indiana University Press.

Basirico, Lawrence A. 1986. "The Art and Craft Fair." *Qualitative Sociology* 9:339–53.

Beamish, Rob. 1982. "Sport and the Logic of Capitalism." In *Sport, Culture, and the Modern State*. Ed. Hart Cantelon and Richard Gruneau. Toronto: University of Toronto Press.

Becker, Howard S. 1960. "Notes on the Concept of Commitment." *American Journal of Sociology* 66:32–40.

– 1982. *Art Worlds*. Berkeley: University of California Press.

Bednarek, Joachim. 1985. "Pumping Iron or Pulling Strings: Different Ways of Working Out and Getting Involved in Body-Building." *International Review of Sport Sociology* 20:239–61.

Begun, James W. 1986. "Economic and Sociological Approaches to Professionalism." *Work and Occupations* 13:113–30.

Bell, Clive. 1958. *Art*. New York: Putnam's.

Bensman, Joseph and Robert Lilienfeld. 1991. *Craft and Consciousness: Occupational Technique and the Development of World Images*, 2d ed. New York: Aldine de Gruyter.

Best, Fred. 1973. "Introduction." In *The Future of Work*. Ed. Fred Best. Englewood Cliffs. NJ: Prentice-Hall.

Bisceglia, Louis. 1980. "Writers of Small Histories: Local Historians in the United States and Britain." *The Local Historian* 14:4–10.

Bishop, Jeff and Paul Hodgett. 1986. *Organizing around Enthusiasms: Mutual Aid in Leisure*. London: Comedia Publishing Group.

Black, Debra. 1991. "Quitting the Rat Race." *Sunday Magazine, Calgary Herald*, 23 June, 26.

Blau, Judith R. 1987. *Architects and Firms*. Cambridge, Mass. MIT Press.

Blau, Judith R. 1988. "Study of the Arts: A Reappraisal." *In Annual Review of Sociology*. Vol. 14. Ed. W. Richard Scott and Judith Blake. Palo Alto, Calif.: Annual Reviews Inc.

Boothby, John and Malcolm F. Tungatt. 1978. "Amateur Sports Clubs: Their Salient Features and Major Advantages." *International Review of Sport Sociology* 4:25–35.

Bosserman, Phillip and R. Gagan. 1972. "Leisure Behavior and Voluntary Action." In *Voluntary Action Research: 1972*. Ed. David H. Smith. Lexington, Mass.: D.C. Heath.

Boutilier, Mary. 1969. "Here's to the Amateur." *Music Journal* 27:62.

Bowen, Catherine Drinker. 1935. *Friends and Fiddlers*. Boston: Little, Brown.

Bowser, Hal. 1978. "Invisible World Sings a Siren to Amateurs." *Smithsonian*, August, 66–72.

Brannigan, Augustine and A.A. McDougall. 1987. "Peril and Pleasure in the Maintenance of a High Risk Sport." In *Sport Sociology*, 3d ed. Ed. Andrew Yiannakis, Thomas D. McIntyre, Merrill J. Melnick, and Dale P. Hart. Dubuque, Iowa: Kendall/Hunt.

Brewer, A. 1979. "Men in the Ranks of Secretaries." *Christian Science Monitor*, February 21, 15.

Bryan, Hobson. 1977. "Leisure Value Systems and Recreational Specialization: The Case of Trout Fishermen." *Journal of Leisure Research* 9:174–87.

– 1979. *Conflict in the Great Outdoors*. Birmingham, Ala.: Bureau of Public Administration, University of Alabama.

Buchanan, Thomas. 1985. "Commitment and Leisure Behavior." *Leisure Sciences* 7:401–20.

Buerkle, Jack V. and Danny Barker. 1973. *Bourbon Street Black: The New Orleans Black Jazzman*. New York: Oxford University Press.

Butler, Robert N. 1977. "The Life Review: An Interpretation of Reminiscence in the Aged." In *Readings in Adult Psychology*. Ed. Lawrence R. Allman and Dennis T. Jaffee. New York: Harper & Row.

Butsch, Richard. 1984. "The Commodification of Leisure: The Case of the Model Airplane Hobby and Industry." *Qualitative Sociology* 7:217–35.

Calgary Herald, 1988. "Volunteers Armed by Worried Police." 25 February, A2.

Calgary Herald. 1990. "Union Chief is Emphasizing Solidarity." 28 February, F3.

Canadian Institute for Public Opinion. 1986. 14 August.

Caplow, Theodore. 1954. *The Sociology of Work*. New York: McGraw-Hill.

Carpenter, Gaylene, Ian Patterson, and Mark Pritchard. In press. "An Investigation of the Relationship between Perceived Freedom in Leisure and Self-Directed Learning." *Schole*.

Carter, Novia. 1975. *Volunteers: The Untapped Potential*. Ottawa: Canadian Council on Social Development.

Cerf. Christopher, and Victor Navasky. 1984. *The Experts Speak: The Definitive Compendium of Authoritative Misinformation*. New York. Pantheon.

Charnofsky, Harold. 1968. "The Major League Professional Baseball Player." *International Review of Sport Sociology* 3:39–55.

Christ, Edwin A. 1965. "The 'Retired' Stamp Collector: Economic and Other Functions of a Systematized Leisure Activity." In *Older People and Their Social World*. Ed. Arnold M. Rose and Warren A. Peterson. Philadelphia, Penn.: F.A. Davis.

Christopherson, Richard W. 1974. "From Folk Art to Fine Art: A Transformation in the Meaning of Photographic Work." *Urban Life and Culture* 3:123–58.

Coakley, Jay J. 1987. "Leaving Competitive Sport: Retirement or Rebirth?" In *Sport Sociology*. 3d ed. Ed. Andrew Yiannakis, Thomas D. McIntyre, Merrill J. Melnick, and Dale P. Hart. Dubuque, Iowa: Kendall/Hunt.

Cohen, Robert. 1990. *Acting Professionally: Raw Facts about Careers in Acting*. 4th ed. Mountain View, Calif.: Mayfield.

Collingwood, R.G. 1958. *The Principles of Art*. New York: Oxford University Press.

Cooper, Patricia and Norma B. Buferd. 1977. *The Quilters: Women and Domestic Art*. Garden City, NY: Doubleday.

Cornwell, Sally C. 1979. "Social and Working Conditions of Artists." *International Labour Review* 118:537–56.

Couch, Stephen R. 1989. "The orchestra as factory." In *Art and Society*. Ed. Arnold W. Foster and Judith R. Blau. Albany, NY: State University of New York Press.

Crane, Diana. 1989. "Reward Systems in Avant-Garde Art: Social Networks and Stylistic Change." In *Art and Society*. Ed. Arnold W. Foster and Judith R. Blau. Albany. NY: State University of New York Press.

Csikszentmihalyi, Mihaly. 1988. "The Flow Experience and Its Significance for Human Psychology." In *Optimal Experience: Psychological Studies of Flow in Consciousness*. Ed. Mihalyi Csikszentmihalyi and Isabella S. Csikszentmihalyi. New York: Cambridge University Press.

Csikszentmihalyi, Mihaly, and Isabella S. Csikszentmihalyi. 1988. *Optimal Experience: Psychological Studies of Flow in Consciousness*. New York: Cambridge University Press.

Curtis, James, and Richard Ennis. 1988. "Negative Consequences of Leaving Competitive Sport? Comparative Findings for Former Elite-Level Hockey Players." *Sociology of Sport Journal* 5:87–106.

Czurles, Stanley A. 1976. "Art Creativity Versus Spectatoritis." *Journal of Creative Behavior* 10:104–7.

Daniels, Arlene K. 1969. "The Captive Professional: Bureaucratic Limitations in the Practice of Military Psychiatry." *Journal of Health and Social Behavior* 10:255–64.

– 1988. *Invisible Careers: Women Civic Leaders from the Volunteer World*. Chicago: University of Chicago Press.

Dannefer, Dale. 1980. "Rationality and Passion in Private Experience: Modern Consciousness and the Social World of Old-Car Collectors." *Social Problems* 27:392–412.

Dawson, Don. 1986. "Unemployment, Leisure, and Liberal-Democratic Ideology." *Loisir et Société* 9:165–82.

Deegan, M.J. and L.E. Nutt. 1975. "The Hospital Volunteer." *Sociology of work and occupations* 2:338–53.

de Grazia, Sebastian. 1962. *Of Time, Work, and Leisure*. New York: Twentieth Century Fund.

de Mille, Agnes. 1952. *Dance to the Piper*. New York: Bantam.

Desautels, Paul E. 1969. *The Mineral Kingdom*. London: The Hamlyn Publishing Group.

Donnelly, Peter and Kevin M. Young. 1985. "Reproduction and Transformation of Cultural Forms in Sport: A Contextual Analysis of Rugby." *International Review for the Sociology of Sport* 20, nos. 1/2:19–38.

Downes, Olin. 1951. "Power to the Public." *New York Times*. Sec. 2 (15 July), 5.

Drinker, Henry S. 1952. "Amateur in Music." *American Philosophical Society Proceedings*. 96:573–7.

– 1967. "Amateur and Music." *Music Educators Journal* 54:75–8.

Dubin, Robert. 1979. "Central Life Interests." *Pacific Sociological Review* 22:405–26.

Duff, Robert W. and Lawrence K. Hong. 1984. "Self-Images of Women bodybuilders." *Sociology of Sport Journal* 1:374–80.

Dumazedier, Joffre. 1967. *Toward a Society of Leisure*. Trans. S.E. McClure. New York: Free Press.

– 1971. "Leisure and Postindustrial Societies." In *Technology, Human Values, and Leisure*. Ed. Max Kaplan and Phillip Bosserman. Nashville, Tenn.: Abington.

– 1974. *Sociology of Leisure*. Amsterdam: Elsevier.

Dunnette, Marvin D., Leaetta Hough, Henry Rosett, Emily Mumford, and Sidney Fine. 1973. "Work and Nonwork." In *Work and Nonwork in the Year 2001*. Ed. Marvin D. Dunnette. Monterey, Calif.: Brooks/Cole.

Edwards, J.M.B. 1968. "Creativity: Social Aspects." In *International Encyclopedia of the Social Sciences*. Vol. 3. Ed. David L. Sills. New York: Collier Macmillan.

Elton, G.R. 1967. *The Practice of History*. New York: Thomas Y. Crowell.

Etzkorn, Peter K. 1973. *Music and Society: The Later Writings of Paul Honigsheim*. New York: Wiley.

Etzkowitz, Henry. 1989. "Entrepreneurial Science in the Academy: A Case of the Transformation of Norms." *Social Problems* 36:14–29.

Ewert, Alan. 1985. "Why People Climb Mountains: The Relationship of Participant Motives and Experience Level to Mountaineering." *Journal of Leisure Research* 17:241–50.

Faulkner, Robert R. 1973. "Career Concerns and Mobility Motivations of Orchestra Musicians." *Sociological Quarterly* 14:334–49.

– 1975. "Coming of Age in Organizations: A Comparative Study of Career Contingencies of Musicians and Hockey Players." In *Sport and Social Order*. Ed. Donald W. Ball and John W. Loy. Reading, Mass.: Addison-Wesley.

– 1976. "Dilemmas in Commercial Work: Hollywood Film Composers and Their Clients." *Urban Life* 5:3–32.

Federico, Ronald C. 1974. "Recruitment, Training, and Performance: The Case of Ballet." In *Varieties of Work Experience*. Ed. Phyllis L. Stewart and Muriel G. Cantor. New York: Wiley.

Finberg, H.P.R. 1967. "Local History." In *Local History*. Ed. H.P.R. Finberg and V.H.T. Skipp. New York: Augustus M. Kelley.

Fine, Gary A. 1979. "Small Groups and Culture Creation." *American Sociological Review* 44:733–45.

– 1983. *Shared Fantasy: Role Playing Games as Social Worlds*. Chicago: University of Chicago Press.

– 1987. "Community and Boundary: Personal Experience Stories of Mushroom Collectors." *Journal of Folklore Research* 24:223–40.

– 1988. "Dying for a Laugh." *Western Folklore* 47:177–94.

– 1989. "Mobilizing Fun: Provisioning Resources in Leisure Worlds." *Sociology of Sport Journal* 6:319–34.

Finnegan, Ruth. 1989. *The Hidden Musicians: Music-Making in an English Town*. Cambridge: Cambridge University Press.

Fisher, Francis D. 1976. "Educating for Underemployment." *Change* 8 (February): 16, 69.

Floro, George K. 1978. "What to look for in a study of the Volunteer in the Work World." In *The Small City and Regional Community*. Ed. R.P. Wolensky and E.J. Miller. Stevens Point, Wisc.: Foundation Press.

– 1983. "The Multi-Dimensional Dairy Goat Industry." Paper presented at the Annual Meeting of the Rural Sociological Society, Lexington, KY.

– 1990. "Voluntary Participation in All Work and Serious Leisure: An Essay Review of *A Gift of Wings* by Richard Bach." *Voluntarism Review and Reporter* 5, no. 1:1–4.

Forsyth, Patrick B., and Thomas J. Danisiewicz. 1985. "Toward a Theory of Professionalization." *Work and Occupations* 12:59–76.

Freidson, Eliot. 1983a. "The Theory of Professions: State of the Art." In *The Sociology of Professions*. Ed. Robert Dingwall and Philip Lewis. London: Macmillan.

– 1983b. "Les professions artistiques comme défi à l'analyse sociologique." *Revue française de sociologie* 27:431–43.

Friedman, Norman L. 1990. "The Hollywood Actor: Occupational Culture, Career, and Adaptation in a Buyers' Market Industry." In *Current Research on Occupations and Professions*. Ed. Helena Z. Lopata. Greenwich, Conn. JAI.

Friedman, Sara Ann. 1986. *Celebrating the Wild Mushroom*. Forestburgh, NY: Lubrecht & Cramer.

Frison, George C. 1984. "Avocational Archaeology." In *Ethics and Values in Archaeology*. Ed. Ernestene L. Green. New York: Free Press.

Frye, J. 1970. "Future of Amateur Radio." *Electronics World* 84:57–8.

Funke, Lewis and John E. Booth (eds.). 1961. *Actors Talk About Acting*. New York: Random House.

Gaev, Dorothy M. 1976. *The Psychology of Loneliness*. Philadelphia. Penn.: Dorothy Meyer Gaev, P.O. Box 27291.

Gans, Herbert J. 1962. "Hollywood Films on British Screens." *Social Problems* 9:324–8.

Garvey, Edward R. 1979. "From Chattel to Employee: The Athlete's Quest for Freedom and Dignity." *The Annals of the American Academy of Political and Social Science* 445 (September): 91–101.

Gelber, Steven M. In press. "Free Market Metaphor: The Historical Dynamics of Stamp Collecting." *Comparative Studies in Society and History*.

– 1991. "A Job You Can't Lose: Work and Hobbies in the Great Depression." *Journal of Social History* 24:741–66.

Getzels, Jacob W., and Mihaly Csikszentmihalyi. 1976. *The Creative Vision: A Longitudinal Study of Problem Finding in Art*, New York: Wiley.

Gibbons, Jacqueline A. 1979. "Artists and Dealers: A Note on the Role of the Art Dealer in the Legitimization of Culture." In *Social Research and Cultural Policy*. Ed. Jiri Zuzanek. Waterloo, Ont.: Otium Publications, University of Waterloo Press.

Gill, C. 1985. *Work, Unemployment and the New Technology*. Oxford: Polity Press.

Glancy, Maureen. 1986. "Participant Observation in the Recreation Setting." *Journal of Leisure Research* 18:59–80.

Glaser, Barney G., ed. 1968. *Organizational Careers: A Sourcebook for Theory*. Chicago: Aldine.

– 1978. *Theoretical Sensitivity*. Mill Valley, CA: The Sociology Press.

Glaser, Barney G. and Anselm L. Strauss. 1967. *The Discovery of Grounded theory*. Chicago: Aldine.

Glasser, Ralph. 1970. *Leisure: Penalty or Prize?* London: Macmillan.

Godbey, Geoffrey. 1990. *Leisure in Your Life*. 3d ed. State College, Penn.: Venture.

Godbout, Jacques. 1986. "La Participation: Instrument de Professionalisation des Loisirs." *Loisir et Société* 9:33–40.

Goffman, Erving. 1963. *Stigma*. Englewood Cliffs, NJ: Prentice-Hall.

Goodman, Calvin J. 1974. "Are You a Professional Artist?" *American Artist* 38 (January): 19–21.

Graefe, Alan R., and Anthony J. Fedler. 1985. "Situated and Subjective Determinants of Satisfaction in Marine Recreational Fishing." *Leisure Sciences* 7:275–98.

Greendorfer, Susan L. and Elaine M. Blinde. 1987. "'Retirement' from Intercollegiate Sports." In *Sport Sociology*. 3d ed. Ed. Andrew Yiannakis, Thomas D. McIntyre, Merrill J. Melnick, and Dale P. Hart. Dubuque, Iowa: Kendall/Hunt.

Greenwood, Ernest. 1957. "Attributes of a Profession." *Social Work* 2:45–55.

Gross, Edward. 1958. *Work and Society*. New York: Thomas Y. Crowell.

Gunn, Scout Lee. 1977. "Labels That Limit Life." *Journal of Physical Education and Recreation* (*Leisure Today* supplement) 27 (October): 3–4.

Gunter, Jay U. 1985. "Asteroids and Amateur Astronomers." *Mercury* (Astronomical Society of the Pacific) 14 (January/February): 9–13, 30.

Hall, Douglas S., Russell M. Genet, and Betty L. Thurston, eds. 1986. *Automatic Photoelectric Telescopes*. Mesa, Ariz.: Fairborn Press.

Hall, Richard H. 1983. "Theoretical Trends in the Sociology of occupations." *Sociological Quarterly* 24:5–23.

– 1986. *Dimensions of Work*. Beverly Hills, Calif.: Sage.

Halpert, Herbert H. and George M. Story, eds. 1969. *Christmas Mumming in Newfoundland*. Toronto: University of Toronto Press.

Hamilton, Lawrence C. 1979. "Modern American Rock Climbing." *Pacific Sociological Review* 22:285–308.

Hanna, Judith L. 1988. *Dance, Sex, and Gender*. Chicago: University of Chicago Press.

Hart, Marie. 1981. "On Being Female in Sport." In *Sport in the Sociocultural Process*. 3d ed. Ed. Marie Hart and Susan Birrell. Dubuque, Iowa: W.C. Brown.

Hastings, Donald W. 1983. "The Ethos of Masters Swimming." *International Review of Sport Sociology* 18, no. 2:31–50.

Hastings, Donald W., Suzanne Kurth, and Judith Meyer. 1989. "Competitive Swimming Careers through the Life Course." *Sociology of Sport Journal* 6:278–84.

Hautaluoma, Jacob, and Perry J. Brown. 1978. "Attributes of the Deer Hunting Experience." *Journal of Leisure Research* 10:271–87.

Hays, Donald S., David R. Genet, and Russell M. Genet, eds. 1987. *New Generation Small Telescopes*. Mesa, Ariz.: Fairborn Press.

Hearle, Rudolf K., Jr. 1975. "Career Patterns and Career Contingencies of Professional Baseball Players." In *Sport and Social Order*. Ed. Donald W. Ball and John W. Loy. Reading, Mass.: Addison-Wesley.

Hearn, Hershel L. 1972. "Aging and the Artistic Career." *The Gerontologist* 12:357–62.

Henderson, Karla A. 1981. "Motivations and Perceptions of Volunteerism as a Leisure Activity." *Journal of Leisure Research* 13:208–18.

Hendrickson, Walter B., 1968. "Speak Up for the Amateur." *Music Journal* 26:34.

Hershon, Marc. 1990. "Just Clowning Around." *Laughtrack* 2 (August): 11–7.

Herskowitz, M. 1972. "Penile Frostbite, an Unforeseen Hazard of Jogging." *New England Journal of Medicine* 296:178.

Hinton-Braaten, Kathleen. 1980. "Symphony Auditions: A Tough Way to Go." *International Musician* 79 (July): 5.

Holtz, Janicemarie A. 1975. "The 'Professional' Duplicate Bridge Player." *Urban Life* 4:131–48.

– 1977. "The Earnest Duplicate Bridge Players." In *Our Sociological Eye*. Ed. Arthur B. Shostak. Port Washington, NY: Alfred.

Homans, George C. 1974. *Social Behavior*. Rev. Ed. New York: Harcourt. Brace, Jovanovich.

Houlston, David R. 1982. "The Occupational Mobility of Professional Athletes." *International Review of Sport Sociology* 17, no. 2:15–28.

Hughes, Everett C. 1971. *The Sociological Eye: Selected Papers on Work, Self, and the Study of Society*. Chicago: Aldine.

Huizinga, Johan. 1955. *Homo Ludens: A Study of the Play Element in Culture*. Boston: Beacon.

Hummel, Richard L. 1985. "Anatomy of a War Game: Target Shooting in Three Cultures." *Journal of Sport Behavior* 8:131–43.

Irwin, John. 1977. *Scenes*. Beverly Hills, Calif.: Sage.

Iso-Ahola, Seppo. 1980. "Toward a Dialectical Social Psychology of Leisure and Recreation." In *Social Psychological Perspectives on Leisure and Recreation*. Ed. Seppo Iso-Ahola. Springfield, Ill.: Charles C. Thomas.

Jackson, Francis. 1967. "The Great Debt We Owe the Gifted Amateur." *Royal School of Church Music News* 17:5.

James, Alan, and Richard Jones. 1982. "The Social World of Karate-Do." *Leisure Studies* 1:337–54.

Jamous, H. and B. Peloille. 1970. "Changes in the French University-Hospital System." In *Professions and Professionalism*. Ed. J.A. Jackson. London: Cambridge University Press.

Jenkins, Clive and Barrie Sherman. 1979. *The Collapse of Work*. London: Eyre Methuen.

Jenner, Jessica R. 1982. "Participation, Leadership and the Role of Volunteerism among Selected Women Volunteers." *Journal of Voluntary Action Research* 11:27–38.

Kamphorst, Teus J. and Marjo Giljam. 1984. "Wind Surfing in Holland." *Leisure Newsletter* 11:24–8.

Kando, Thomas M. 1980. *Leisure and Popular Culture in Transition*. 2d ed. St. Louis, Mo.: C.V. Mosby.

Kantor, Rosabeth M. 1969. "Commitment and Social Organization." *American Sociological Review* 33:499–517.

Kaplan, Max. 1955. *Music in Recreation.* Champaign, Ill.: Stipes.

– 1960. *Leisure in America.* New York: Wiley.

– 1975. *Leisure: Theory and Policy.* New York: Wiley.

Kellert, Stephen R. 1985. "Birdwatching in American Society." *Leisure Sciences* 7:343–60.

Kelley, Jane. 1963. "Some thoughts on Amateur Archaeology." *American Antiquity* 28:394–6.

Kelly, John R. 1974. "Sociological Perspectives and Leisure Research." *Current Sociology* 22:127–58.

– 1983. *Leisure Identities and Interactions.* Boston: George Allen & Unwin.

– 1987. "The Arts in the United States of America." In *Trends in the Arts: A Multinational Perspective.* Ed. Linda Hantrais and Teus J. Kamphorst. The Netherlands: Giordano Bruno Press.

Kelly, John R., and Jo-Ellen Ross. 1989. "Later-Life Leisure: Beginning a New Agenda." *Leisure Sciences* 11:47–59.

Kenyon, Gerald S. and Barry D. McPherson. 1981. "Becoming Involved in Physical Activity and Sport." In *Sport, Culture, and Society.* 2d ed. Ed. John W. Loy, Gerald S. Kenyon, and Barry D. McPherson. Philadelphia, Pa.: Lea & Febiger.

Klegon, Douglas. 1978. "The Sociology of Professions: An Emerging perspective." *Sociology of Work and Occupations* 5:259–83.

Kleiber, Douglas, Susan Greendorfer, Elaine Blinde, and Diane Samdahl. 1987. "Quality of Exit from University Sports and Life Satisfaction in Early Adulthood." *Sociology of Sport Journal* 4:28–36.

Klein, Alan M. 1985. "Muscle Manor." *Journal of Sport and Social Issues* 9:4–19.

Klein, John F. 1974. "Professional Theft: The Utility of a Concept." *Canadian Journal of Criminology and Corrections* 16:133–44.

Kohansky, Mendel. 1984. *The Disreputable Profession: The actor in society.* Westport, Conn.: Greenwood.

Krucoff, Carol. 1990. "Exercise and Romance: How Your Workouts Affect the One You Love." *Washington Post*, 13 February, 18.

Kutner, Nancy G. 1983. "The Touring Tennis Player." In *Research in the Sociology of Work.* Ed. Ida W. Simpson and Richard L. Simpson. Greenwich, Conn.: JAI.

Lacroix, Jean-Guy. 1990. *La condition d'artiste: une injustice.* Outremont, Qué. VLB Editeur.

Langton, Arthur. 1932. "Anti-Social Aspects of Golf." *Sociology and Social Research* 17:55–61.

Lankford, John. 1979. "Amateur Versus Professional: The Transatlantic Debate over the Measure of Jovian longitude." *Journal of the British Astronomical Association* 89:574–82.

– 1981a. "Amateurs and Astrophysics: A neglected Aspect of the Development of a Scientific Speciality." *Social Studies of Science* 11:275–303.

– 1981b. "Amateurs versus Professionals: The Controversy over Telescope Size in Late Victorian Science." *Isis* 72:11–28.

Lauffer, Armand and Sarah Gorodezky. 1977. *Volunteers*. Beverly Hills, Calif.: Sage.

Lefkowitz, Bernard. 1979. *Breaktime*. New York: Penguin.

Levy, Emanuel. 1989. "The Choice of Acting as a Profession." In *Art and Society*. Ed. Arnold W. Foster and Judith R. Blau. Albany, NY: State University of New York Press.

Lewis, Lionel S. 1982. "Working at Leisure: Businessmen in Search of the Good Life." *Society/Transaction* 19 (July/August): 27–32.

Lifton, Robert J. 1977. "The Sense of Immortality: On Death and the Continuity of Life." In *New Meanings of Death*. Ed. Herman Feifel. New York: McGraw-Hill.

Lopreato, Joseph and Letitia Alston. 1970. "Ideal Types and the Idealization Strategy." *American Sociological Review* 35:88–96.

Lyman, Stanford and Marvin B. Scott. 1989. *A Sociology of the Absurd*. 2d ed. Dix Hills, NJ: General Hall.

Lyon, Eleanor. 1974. "Work and Play: Resource Constraints in a Small Theater." *Urban Life and Culture* 3:71–97.

– 1982. "Stages of Theatrical Rehearsal." *Journal of Popular Culture* 16 (Fall): 75–89.

Macbeth, Jim. 1988. "Ocean Cruising." In *Optimal Experience: Psychological Studies of Flow in Consciousness*. Ed. Mihalyi Csikszentmihalyi and Isabella S. Csikszentmihalyi. New York: Cambridge University Press.

McPherson, Barry D., James E. Curtis, and John W. Loy. 1989. *The Social Significance of Sport*. Champaign. Ill.: Human Kinetics.

Mahoney, Michael J. 1976. *Scientist as Subject: The Psychological Imperative*. Cambridge, Mass.: Ballinger.

Manning, Peter K. and Hershel L. Hearn. 1969. "Student Actresses and Their Artistry." *Social Forces* 48:202–13.

Margoshes, David. 1979. "Rodeo Cowboys Branded as 'Wild West' Amateurs." *Calgary Herald*, 21 March, C2.

Marsh, Leonard. 1972. *At Home With Music*. Vancouver: Versatile Publishing Co.

Maslow, Abraham. 1954. *Motivation and Personality*. New York: Harper & Row.

Maunsell, T.A.K. 1963. "Amateur Music Societies, 1935 to 1962." *Making Music* 51:10–1.

Mayfield, Harold F. 1979. "The Amateur in Ornithology." *The Auk* 96:168–71.

Mayr, Ernest. 1975. "Materials for an American Ornithology." In *Ornithology: From Aristotle to the Present*. Ed. Erwin Streseman. Cambridge, Mass.: Harvard University Press.

Meier, Gretl S. 1979. *Job Sharing*. Kalamazoo, Mich.: Upjohn Institute for Employment Research.

Merrill, Francis E. 1970. "Le Groupe des Batignolles: A Study in the Sociology of Art." In *Human Nature and Collective Behavior*. Ed. Tamotsu Shibutani. Englewood Cliffs. NJ: Prentice-Hall.

Miller, Delbert C., and William H. Form. 1980. *Industrial Sociology*. 3d ed. New York: Harper & Row.

Mitchell, Richard G., Jr. 1983. *Mountain Experience*. Chicago: University of Chicago Press.

Monthly Labor Review. 1990. 113 (July): 61.

Moore, S., and J. Viorst, eds. 1961. *Wonderful World of Science*. New York, Bantam.

Mulac, Margaret E. 1977. "Retirement and Leisure." *Journal of Physical Education and Recreation (Leisure Today* supplement) 27 (October): 18.

Mullen, Ken. 1985. "The Impure Performance Frame of the Public House entertainer." *Urban Life* 14:181–205.

Music Calgary. 1988. October, 2.

Musical America. 1951. "Amateur Orchestra." 71, September, 11.

Nardi, Peter M. 1983. "A Social Psychological Profile of Amateur and professional magicians." Department of Sociology, Pitzer College, Claremont, Calif.

– 1988. "The Social World of Magicians: Gender and conjuring." *Sex Roles* 19:759–70.

Nash, Jeffrey E. 1979. "Weekend Racing as an Eventful Experience." *Urban Life* 8:199–217.

National Advisory Council on Voluntary Action. 1978. *People in Action*. Ottawa: Minister of Supply and Services.

Neulinger, John. 1981. *The Psychology of Leisure*. 2d ed. Springfield, Ill.: Charles C. Thomas.

Newman, Peter C. 1983. "Defining the New Ambition." *Financial Post Magazine*, 1 September, 12.

New York Times, 1959. "Letter to the Editor," Section 2, 8 March:9.

Ng, David and Leslie June. 1985. "Electronic Leisure and Youth: Kitchener Arcade Video Game Players." *Society and Leisure* 8:537–48.

Noble, Richard D.C. 1970. "The Great Divide." *Bulletin* (The Dolmetsch Foundation), 16 (March): 2.

Olmsted, Allan D. 1987. "Stamp Collectors and Stamp Collecting." Paper presented at the annual meeting of the Popular Culture Association, March, Montreal.

– 1988. "Morally Controversial Leisure: The Social World of the Gun Collector." *Symbolic Interaction* 11:277–87.

Olmsted, Allan D., and Jarmila Horna. 1989. "Pin Trading at the 1988 Calgary Winter Olympics." Paper presented at the annual meeting of the Popular Culture Association, March, St. Louis, Mo.

Orzack, Louis H. 1959. "Work as a 'Central Life Interest' of Professionals." *Social Problems* 7:125–31.

Parade. 1975, 16.

Parker, Stanley. 1971. *The Future of Work and Leisure.* New York: Praeger.

– 1974. "Professional Life and Leisure." *New Society* 30, 10 October, 77–8.

– 1983. *Leisure and Work.* London: George Allen & Unwin.

– 1987a. "Volunteering as Serious Leisure in Britain and Australia." Paper presented at the Leisure Research Symposium. Eastbourne, England.

– 1987b. "Working for Peace as Serious Leisure." *Leisure Information Quarterly* 13, no. 4:9–10.

Parliament, Jo-Anne B. 1989. "How Canadians Spend Their Day." *Canadian Social Trends* 15 (Winter): 23–7.

Parmenter, Ross. 1962. "Pros versus Amateurs in Fort Wayne Row." *New York Times,* Section 2, 4 November, 11.

Parsons, Talcott. 1968. "Professions." In *International Encyclopedia of the Social Sciences.* Vol. 12. Ed. David L. Sills. New York: Crowell, Collier, Macmillan.

Pavalko, Ronald M. 1988. *Sociology of Occupations and Professions.* 2d ed. Itasca, Ill.: F.E. Peacock.

Pawluk, Anne. 1984. "The Status and Style of Life of Polish Olympians after Completion of Their Sports Careers." *International Review of Sport Sociology* 19:169–83.

Pearson, Kent. 1980. *Surfing Subcultures.* Lawrence, Mass.: University of Queensland Press.

Perreault, Michel. 1988. "La passion et le corps comme objets de la sociologie: la dance comme carrière." *Sociologie et Société* 20:177–86.

Perry, Bliss. 1904. *The Amateur Spirit.* Freeport, NY: Books for Libraries Press.

Piscator, Erwin. 1949. "Objective Acting." In *Actors on Acting.* Ed. Toby Cole and Helen K. Chinoy. New York: Crown.

Podilchak, Walter, 1986. "Fun is Social." PH.D. diss., Department of Sociology, University of Calgary.

– 1988. "Establishing the Fun in Leisure." Paper presented at the World Congress on Free time, Culture, and Society, May, Lake Louise, Alberta, Canada.

– 1989. "Solitary and Interactive Fun Experiences." *World Leisure and Recreation* 31 (Fall): 15–17.

Portwood, Derek, and Alan Fielding. 1981. "Privilege and the Professions." *Sociological Review* 29:749–73.

Prus, Robert C., and C.R.D. Sharper. 1991. *Road Hustler: Grifting, Magic, and the Thief Subculture,* expanded ed. New York: Kaufman and Greenberg.

Ramsey, Frederick. Jr. 1970. *Where the Music Started.* New Brunswick. NJ: Institute of Jazz Studies, Rutgers University.

Randi, James. 1978. "The Psychology of Conjuring." *Technology Review* 80, no. 3:56–63.

Reeves, Joy B. 1986. "The Survival Game: Who Plays and Why." *Sociology of Sport Journal* 3:57–61.

Riley, Matilda W., Anne Foner, and Joan Waring. 1988. "Sociology of Age." In *Handbook of Sociology*. Ed. Neil J. Smelser. Newbury Park, Calif.: Sage.

Ritzer, George, and David Walczak. 1986. *Working: Conflict and Change*. 3d ed. Englewood Cliffs. NJ: Prentice-Hall.

Roadburg, Alan. 1976. "Is Professional Football a Profession?" *International Review of Sport Sociology* 11:27–37.

– 1985. *Aging: Retirement, Leisure, and Work in Canada*. Toronto: Methuen.

Robbins, James M., and Paul Joseph. 1980. "Commitment to Running: Implications for Family and Work." *Sociological Symposium* 30:7–108.

Roberts, Brian A. 1991a. *A Place to Play: The Social World of University Music Students*. St. John's, Nfld.: Faculty of Education, Memorial University of Newfoundland.

– 1991b. *Musician: A Process of Labelling*. St. John's, Nfld.: Faculty of Education, Memorial University of Newfoundland.

Roberts, Kenneth. 1981. "Leisure, Work and Education." Bletchley, England: Open University Press. E 200, Block 5.

Robinson, B.W., and E.D. Salamon. 1987. "Gender Role Socialization: A Review of the Literature," In *Gender Roles*. Ed. E.D. Salamon and B.W. Robinson. Toronto: Methuen.

Robinson, John P., and Geoffrey Godbey. 1978. "Work and Leisure in America: How We Spend Our Time." *Journal of Physical Education and Health* (*Leisure Today* supplement) 49:6–7.

Rojek, Chris. 1987. "Freedom, Power and Leisure." *Loisir et Société* 10:209–18.

Rosenberg, Bernard, and Norris Fliegel. 1965. *The Vanguard Artist*. Chicago: Quadrangle.

Rosenberg, Bernard, and Norris Fliegel. 1970. "The Artist and His Publics." In *The Sociology of Art and Literature*. Ed. Milton C. Albrecht, James H. Barnett, and Mason Griff. New York: Praeger.

Rosenblum, Barbara. 1978. *Photographers at Work: A Sociology of Photographic Styles*. New York: Holmes & Meier.

Roth. Julius A. 1974. "Professionalism: The Sociologist's Decoy." *Sociology of Work and Occupations* 1:6–23.

Rothenberg, Marc. 1981. "Organization and Control: Professionals and Amateurs in American Astronomy." *Social Studies in Science* 11:305–25.

Saks, Mike. 1983. "Removing the Blinkers? A Critique of Recent Contributions to the Sociology of Professions." *Sociological Review* 31:1–21.

Sanders, Clinton R. 1974. "Psyching Out the Crowd: Folk Performers and Their Audiences." *Urban Life and Culture* 3:264–82.

Schwartz, Dona. 1986. "Camera Clubs and Fine Art Photography." *Urban Life* 15:165–95.

Seabrook, Jeremy. 1973. *Loneliness*. London: Temple Smith.

Selnow, Gary. 1987. "The Rise and Fall of Video Games." *Journal of Popular Culture* 21 (Summer): 53–62.

Seltzer, George. 1989. *Music Matters: The Performer and the American Federation of Musicians.* Metuchen, NJ: Scarecrow Press.

Seltzer, Joseph, and John A. Wilson. 1980. "Leisure Patterns among Four-Day Workers." *Journal of Leisure Research* 12:116–27.

Senters, Jo. M. 1971. "A Function of Uncertainty and Stakes in Recreation." *Pacific Sociological Review* 14:259–69.

Shamir, Boas. 1985. "Unemployment and 'Free Time' – The Role of the Protestant Work Ethic and Work Involvement." *Leisure Studies* 4:333–45.

– 1988. "Commitment and Leisure." *Sociological Perspectives* 31:238–58.

Shaw, Susan M. 1985. "The Meaning of Leisure in Everyday Life." *Leisure Sciences* 7:1–24.

Sherman, Barrie. 1986. *Working at Leisure.* London: Methuen.

Simpson, Charles R. 1981. *SoHo: The Artist in the City.* Chicago: University of Chicago Press.

– 1989. "Shadows of Anxiety: Popular Culture in Modern Society." In *Art and Society.* Ed. Arnold W. Foster and Judith R. Blau. Albany, NY: State University of New York.

Sinha, Anita. 1979. "Control in Craft Work: The Case of Production Potters." *Qualitative Sociology* 2:3–25.

Slovenko, Ralph, and James A. Knight, eds. 1967. *Motivation in Play, Games, and Sports.* Springfield, Ill.: Charles C. Thomas.

Smith, David H. 1975. "Voluntary Action and Voluntary Groups." In *Annual Review of Sociology.* Vol. 1. Ed. Alex Inkeles, James Coleman, and Neil Smelser. Palo Alto, Calif. Annual Reviews Inc.

Smith, Stephen L.J. 1979. "The Relationship Between Active and Passive Involvement in the Arts – Is the Artist Also a Spectator?" In *Social Research and Cultural Policy.* Ed. Jiri Zuzanek. Waterloo, Ont.: Otium Publication, University of Waterloo.

Snyder, Eldon E. 1986. "The Social World of Shuffleboard: Participation among Senior Citizens." *Urban Life* 15:237–53.

Snyder, Eldon E., and Elmer A. Spreitzer. 1989. *Social Aspects of Sport.* 3d ed. Englewood Cliffs. NJ: Prentice-Hall.

Spreitzer, Elmer, and Eldon E. Snyder. 1983. "Correlates of Participation in Adult Recreational Sports." *Journal of Leisure Research* 15:27–38.

Standing Committee on Communications and Culture. 1989. "Minutes of Proceedings and Evidence of the Sub-Committee on the Status of the Artist," Issue no. 1. Ottawa: House of Commons, Government of Canada.

Statistics Canada. 1980. *An Overview of Volunteer Workers in Canada.* Cat. no. 71–530. Ottawa.

– 1990. *The Labour Force.* Cat. no. 71–001. Ottawa.

Stebbins, Robert A. 1962. "The Conflict between Musical and Commercial Values in the Minneapolis Jazz Community." *Proceedings of the Minnesota Academy of Science* 30:75–9.

– 1968. "A Theory of the Jazz Community." *Sociological Quarterly* 9:318–31.

– 1969. "Role Distance, Role-Distance Behaviour, and Jazz Musicians." *British Journal of Sociology* 20:405–15.

– 1970a. "Career: The Subjective Approach." *Sociological Quarterly* 11:32–49.

– 1970b. "On Misunderstanding the Concept of Commitment." *Social Forces* 48:526–9.

– 1971. *Commitment to Deviance: The Nonprofessional Criminal in the Community.* Westport, Conn.: Greenwood.

– 1976. "Music among Friends: The Social Networks of Amateur Classical Musicians." *International Review of Sociology* (Series II) 12:52–73.

– 1977. "The Amateur: Two Sociological Definitions." *Pacific Sociological Review* 20:582–606.

– 1978a. "Toward Amateur Sociology: A Proposal for the Profession." *The American Sociologist* 13:239–47.

– 1978b. "Classical Music Amateurs: A Definitional Study." *Humboldt Journal of Social Relations* 5:78–103.

– 1978c. "Creating High Culture: The American Amateur Classical Musician." *Journal of American Culture* 1:616–31.

– 1979a. *Amateurs: On the Margin between Work and Leisure.* Beverly Hills, Calif.: Sage.

– 1979b. "Family, Work, and Amateur Acting." In *Social Research and Cultural Policy.* Ed. Jiri Zuzanek. Waterloo, Ont.: Otium Publications, University of Waterloo.

– 1980. "Avocational Science: The Avocational Routine in Archaeology and Astronomy." *International Journal of Comparative Sociology* 21:34–48.

– 1981a. "Toward a Social Psychology of Stage Fright." In *Sport in the Sociocultural Process.* Ed. Marie Hart and Susan Birrell. Dubuque, Iowa: W.C. Brown.

– 1981b. "Science *Amators*? Rewards and Costs in Amateur Astronomy and Archaeology." *Journal of Leisure Research* 13:289–304.

– 1982a. "Serious Leisure: A Conceptual Statement." *Pacific Sociological Review* 25:251–72.

– 1982b. "Amateur and Professional Astronomers: A Study of Their Inter-relationships." *Urban Life* 10:433–54.

– 1984. *The Magician: Career, Culture, and Social Psychology in a Variety Art.* Toronto: Irwin.

– 1987a. *Canadian Football: The View from the Helmet.* London, Ont.: Centre for Social and Humanistic Studies. University of Western Ontario.

– 1987b. "Professional-Amateur Relations as a Neglected Dimension in the Study of Occupations: The Case of Entertainment Magic." In *Current*

Research on Occupations and Professions. Ed. Helena Z. Lopata. Greenwich, Conn.: JAI.

– 1990. *The Laugh-Makers: Stand-Up Comedy as Art, Business, and Life-Style*. Montreal and Kingston: McGill-Queen's University Press.

– 1991. "Hobbies as Marginal Leisure: The Case of Barbershop Singers." *Loisir et Société* 14:

– 1992. "Becoming a Barbershop Singer." In *Barbershopping, Popular Culture, and Leisure*. Ed. Max Kaplan. Madison, NJ: Fairleigh Dickinson University Press.

– In press. "Costs and Rewards of Barbershop Singing." *Leisure Studies*.

Stenross, Barbara. 1990. "Turning Vices into Virtues: The Dignifying Accounts of Gun Avocationists." In *Marginal Conventions: Popular Culture, Mass Media, and Social Deviance*. Ed. Clinton R. Sanders. Bowling Green, Ohio: Bowling State University Popular Press.

Stone, Gregory P. 1972. "American Sports: Play and Display." In *Sport*. Ed. Eric Dunning. Toronto: University of Toronto Press.

Strauss, Anselm L. 1987. *Qualitative Analysis for Social Scientists*. New York: Cambridge University Press.

Sudnow, David. 1978. *Ways of the Hand: The Organization of Improvised Conduct*. New York: Harper & Row.

Super, Donald E. 1957. *The Psychology of Careers*. New York: Harper & Row.

Sutherland, David E. 1989. "Ballet as a Career." In *Art and Society*. Ed. Arnold W. Foster and Judith R. Blau. Albany, NY: State University of New York.

Swezey, Kenneth M. 1948. *After-Dinner Science*. New York: McGraw-Hill.

Task Force on Employment Opportunities for the 80s. 1982. *Work for Tomorrow: Employment Opportunities for the 80s*. Cat. no. XC2-321/4–01E. Ottawa: Speaker of the House of Commons.

Taylor, John F.A. 1964–6. "Comment." *Arts in Society* 3:18.

Tess, Kay. 1990. "Active Unemployment – A Leisure Pattern for the Future?" *Loisir et Société* 12:413–30.

Theberge, Nancy. 1977. "An Occupational Analysis of Women's Professional Golf." PH.D. diss. Department of Sociology, University of Massachusetts, Amhurst, Mass.

– 1980. "The System of Rewards in Women's Professional Golf." *International Review of Sport Sociology* 15, no. 2:27–42.

Thompson, Paul D., Michael P. Stern, Paul Williams, Kirk Duncan, William L. Haskell, and Peter D. Wood. 1979. "Death during Jogging or Running: A Study of 18 Cases." *Journal of the American Medical Association* 242, no. 12:1265–7.

Thurston, Harry. 1988. "Nova Scotia Traditions." *Equinox* 39:49–57.

Todd, Elizabeth. 1930. "Amateur." In *Encyclopedia of the Social Sciences*. vol. 2. Ed. R.A. Seligman. New York: Macmillan.

Toffler, Alvin. 1964. *The Culture Consumers*. New York: Random House.

Toles, Terri. 1985. "Video Games and American Military Ideology." *Arena Review* 9 (March): 58–76.

Tomars, Adolph S. 1964–6. "The Citizen in the Roles of Producer and Consumer of Art." *Arts in Society* 3:45–55.

Truzzi, Marcello. 1978. "Toward a General Sociology of the Folk, Popular, and Elite Arts." In *Research in Sociology of Knowledge, Sciences, and Art*. Vol. 1. Ed. Robert A. Jones. Greenwich, Conn.: JAI.

Turnbaugh, William A., Christian L. Vanderbroek, and Janet S. Jones. 1983. "The Professionalism of Amateurs in Archaeology." *Archaeology* 36, no. 6:22–9.

US Bureau of the Census. 1988. *Statistical Abstract of the United States: 1988*. 108th ed. Washington, DC.

US National Institute of Law Enforcement and Criminal Justice. 1977. *Citizen Patrol Projects: National Evaluation Program*. Washington, DC: US Government Printing Office.

Unruh, David R. 1980. "The Nature of Social Worlds." *Pacific Sociological Review* 23:271–96.

– 1983. *Invisible Lives: The Social Worlds of the Aged*. Beverly Hills, Calif.: Sage.

Van Til, Jon. 1988. *Mapping the Third Sector: Voluntarism in a Changing Political Economy*. New York: The Foundation Center.

Vaughn, Paul. 1959. "The Music Makers." *The Spectator* (London) 202, 8 May, 647–8.

Veal, A.J. 1987. *Leisure and the Future*. London: Allen & Unwin.

Wall, Richard. 1984. "Harnessing Leisure to Research: English Local History." *Economic and Social Research Council Bulletin* 51 (March): 25–7.

Walters, Vivian. 1982. "Company Doctors' Perceptions of and Responses to Conflicting Pressures from Labor and Management." *Social Problems* 30:1–12.

Wardwell, Walter I. 1952. "A Marginal Professional Role: The chiropractor." *Social Forces* 30:339–48.

Waters, Malcolm. 1989. "Collegiality, Bureaucratization, and Professionalization: A Weberian Analysis." *American Journal of Sociology* 94:945–79.

Watson, Stuart W., Michael H. Legg, and Joy B. Reeves. 1980. "The Enduro Dirt-Bike Rider." *Leisure Sciences* 3:241–56.

Watson, W.Y. 1975. "On Amateur Entomology." *Entomological Society of Canada Bulletin* 7:34.

Wayne, Jamie. 1990. "Pedal Power." *Financial Post*, 17 September, 11.

Weber, Max. 1968. *Max Weber on Charisma and Institution Building*. Ed. S.N. Eisenstadt. Chicago: University of Chicago Press.

Weiss, Paul. 1969. *Sport: A Philosophic Inquiry*. Carbondale. Ill.: University of Southern Illinois Press.

Westby, David L. 1960. "The Career Experience of the Symphony Musician." *Social Forces* 38:223–30.

Whannel, Garry. 1983. *Blowing the Whistle: The Politics of Sport*. London: Pluto Press.

White, Stephen W. 1982. "Leisure as a Social Issue." *National Forum* 62 (Summer): 2.

Wilensky, Harold L. 1964. "The Professionalization of Everyone." *American Journal of Sociology* 70:137–58.

Williams, Thomas R. 1983. "Astronomers as Amateurs." *The Journal of the American Association of Variable Star Observers* 12:1–4.

– 1987. "Criteria for Classifying an Astronomer as an Amateur." Paper presented at the International Astronomical Union Colloquium 98, June, Paris.

Williams, Trevor, and Peter Donnelly. 1985. "Subcultural Production, Reproduction, and Transformation in Climbing." *International Review for the Sociology of Sport* 20, nos. 1/2: 3–17.

Williams, Joyce, L. 1987. "An Uneasy Balance: Voluntarism and Professionalism." *American Archivist* 50 (Winter): 7–10.

Wilson, John. 1980. "Sociology of Leisure." In *Annual Review of Sociology*. Vol. 6. Ed. Alex Inkeles, Neil J. Smelser, and Ralph H. Turner. Palo Alto, Calif.: Annual Reviews.

– 1988. *Politics and Leisure*. London: Allen & Unwin.

Wilson, Robert N. 1964. "The Poet in American Society." In *The Arts in Society*. Ed. Robert N. Wilson. Englewood Cliffs. NJ: Prentice-Hall.

Woolgar, Steve. 1988. *Science: The Very Idea*. Sussex: Ellis Horwood.

Yair, Gad. 1990. "The Commitment to Long-Distance Running and Level of Activities." *Journal of Leisure Research* 22:213–27.

Yankelovich, Daniel. 1981. *New Rules: Searching for Self-Fulfillment in a World Turned Upside Down*. New York: Random House.

Yates, Peter. 1964–6. "Amateur Versus Professional." *Arts in Society* 3:19–24.

Zimmer, Carl. 1990. "Amateur Night." *Discover* 11 (December): 59–61.

Zimmerman, Kate. 1982. "Club Offers Young Writers New Chance." *Calgary Herald*, 25 November, G8.

Zuckerman, Harriet, and Robert K. Merton. 1971. "Patterns of Evaluation in Science: Institutionalisation, Structure, and Functions of the Referee System." *Minerva* 9:66–100.

Zurcher, Louis A., and Gwyn Harries-Jenkins. 1978. *Supplementary Military Forces: Reserves, Militias, and Auxiliaries*. Beverly Hills, Calif.: Sage.

Zuzanek, Jiri. 1978. *Artist in Contemporary Society: Praise Without Pay?* Research Group on Leisure and Cultural Development. Research Paper no. 1. Waterloo, Ont.: University of Waterloo.

Author Index

Subject Index

Accomplishment, sense of, 7, 17, 95, 98, 125, 126–7, 128–9; and life review, 129

Activity participants (*see also* Hobbyist pursuits), 12–13

Acting: and marital breakup, 109; disappointments in, 101; dislikes in, 102–10; stage fright in, 50

Aging. *See* Retirement

Altruism, 16, 18

Amateur pursuits (*see also* Amateurs; Arts, the; Entertainment; Science; Serious leisure; Sport), 8–10; and avocational collectivism, 78; as avocations, 122; and conflict with work, 112–13, 139; as contributions to culture, 16–18; as contributions to the community, 118–120, 121–2; as delegated tasks, 138; as differentiated from hobbyism and volunteering, 18; and economic individualism, 96; and entrepreneurship, 78–80; and harmony with work, 113–14; marginality of,

37, 55–7, 58, 108, 120–2, 141; modern, rise of, 10, 14–15, 137; remuneration from, 5, 11, 58, 60, 79–80, 95, 98; in retirement, 127; self-interest and, 16, 18, 96; seriousness of, 55–6; sociological study of, 10, 37; and the media, 117; uncontrollability of, 56

Amateurs (*see also* Amateur pursuits; Arts, the; Careers; Entertainment; Science; Serious leisure; Sport), 38–58; ambivalence of, 121; as adults, 41; as *amators*, 43–5, 93; as collectors, 137; as conditional preprofessionals, 46–7; definition of, xi, 10, 20, 41–6, 48–55, 57–8, 134, 137, 138, 140; as deviant, 56; as devotees, 46–8, 82, 140; differentiated from professionals by attitude, 48–55; frustration of, 57; "gentlemen," 9, 14, 42, 137; as participants, 46–8, 82, 140; as part of a public, 59; as postprofessionals, 46, 48, 90, 91; as pre-professionals,

46–8, 81–2; professional attributes applied to, 25, 31, 38; professional standards of, 57; as pure amateurs, 46; and social class, 9–10, 111–12; students as, 47; and the community, 108–22; types of, 46–8; and types of relations with professionals, 114–16; and work roles, 41

Archaeology: remuneration for amateurs in, 60

Arts, the fine (*see also* Amateurs; Careers; Costs; Professionals; Publics): amateur-professional relations in, 115–16; assessment (audition, jury) in, 85, 88, 103, 105; commercialism in, 85; creative decline in, 91; entrepreneurship in, 78–80; financial insecurity in, 106; Marx's view of, 132; obsolescence in, 91; onstage predicaments in, 106–7

Astronomy: career entry for amateurs in, 72; careers in PAP system of, 41; disappointments in, 101; dislikes in, 102; and